Twayne's United States Authors Series

EDITOR OF THIS VOLUME

Sylvia E. Bowman

Indiana University

H. L. Davis

TUSAS 306

H. L. Davis

H. L. DAVIS

By PAUL T. BRYANT

Colorado State University

TWAYNE PUBLISHERS
A DIVISION OF G. K. HALL & CO., BOSTON

Library of Congress Cataloging in Publication Data

Bryant, Paul T
  H. L. Davis.

  (Twayne's United States authors series ; TUSAS 306)
  Bibliography: p. 161 - 68
  Includes index.
  1.   Davis, Harold Lenoir, 1894 - 1960—Criticism and interpreta-
tion.
PS3507.A7327Z62   1978   ~~813'.5'2~~   77-25525
ISBN 0-8057-7211-1

For Genny

Contents

About the Author

Born in Oklahoma in 1928, grandson of a homesteader on the Western prairie, Paul Bryant has had a lifelong association with the literature and history of the American West. Working as a farm and ranch hand on the High Plains in his adolescent years, he has since held summer jobs in the West with the National Park Service, the Forest Service, and the Audubon Society. After service in the army, he graduated from the University of Oklahoma with master's degrees in both plant ecology and in English. He worked as an engineering and science writer and editor at Washington State University and the University of Illinois and served as editor of the *Journal of Engineering Education* from 1958 to 1964. He received his doctorate in English from the University of Illinois in 1965.

Dr. Bryant served as an assistant editor of *Western American Literature* from its founding in 1966 until 1971. Co-founder of the *Journal of English Teaching Techniques* in 1967, he has continued on that journal's editorial board. Compiler and editor of *From Geography to Geotechnics*, selected essays of Benton MacKaye, Dr. Bryant has published articles on American literature, composition, pedagogy, environmentalism, and on the relationship between environmentalism and American literature, as well as poetry and fiction. A Professor of English at Colorado State University, he is currently engaged in research on the family history as a folk literature in the American West.

Preface

H. L. Davis has been recognized repeatedly as a writer of major significance. His work has been compared favorably with that of such writers as Twain, Steinbeck, and Faulkner. It has won prizes and praise from some of the leading writers and critics in this country. Yet for the most part critics have ignored Davis, and there has been no extended critical examination of his achievement. This volume is an attempt to remedy that deficiency and to call attention to the significance of Davis's work.

Critical neglect of Davis's work seems to stem from a variety of causes. Perhaps a major factor is that most of his work is set in the American West in the nineteenth century and early twentieth century. Only in the last few years, with recognition of the artistic stature of such writers as Walter Van Tilburg Clark and Wallace Stegner, has the literary establishment been willing to treat writers of the American West seriously. Adding to this difficulty was Davis's intriguing personal combination of shyness and iconoclasm which kept him from joining fashionable literary coteries or forming useful literary connections. He was an inveterate maverick who ignored artistic and intellectual fashions.

My primary objective has been to provide basic interpretive readings of representative poems, the best of his short prose, and all five of the novels. Because most of Davis's work is currently out of print, these readings are accompanied by extended plot outlines for all of the novels and summaries for those short stories and sketches discussed. These readings are intended to show the primary patterns and techniques through which Davis developed his art and presented his vision of the universal human condition as exemplified in the life of the American West.

A second objective has been to establish the basic biographical facts about Davis, without attempting a fully developed biography. Biographical information about Davis has been confused and contradictory almost from the beginning of his writing career. A biographer is confronted by a tangle of birth dates ranging from 1894 to 1904, by cryptic references to a kaleidoscope of experiences that could not possibly have been packed into the few years assigned to them, and by references to his family that are just as confusing and contradictory. These puzzles come primarily from information supplied at various times by Davis himself. The problem is compounded by the absence of birth records in Davis's home area in the 1890s and by the loss to fire of his public-school records. Nevertheless, the major facts of Davis's life have emerged from existing records, from journals and correspondence, and from consultation with surviving relatives and friends.

A third objective has been to present a summary and discussion of the critical reception at the time of publication of each of Davis's novels. This treatment seemed desirable because, as a writer of the American West, Davis labored under certain handicaps that affected both the reception and the understanding of his work. Explanations may be found in this presentation for many of the paradoxes of recognition and neglect in Davis's writing career. More broadly, this examination of the critical reception of Davis's work provides a general paradigm for the problems of critical reception of most other significant American writers whose work has been set in the West.

H. L. Davis was an artistic loner. He knew thoroughly and worked very consciously from the literary tradition of our culture, but he kept himself separate from cliques and movements, followed his own path of artistic development, and evolved a highly individual style and technique. For this reason, it has not seemed necessary to relate his career in any elaborate or extended way to the literary movements of his time. Instead, I have tried to focus directly on his work. That is what deserves to be better understood. That is what will survive in the canon of American literature.

PAUL T. BRYANT

Colorado State University

Acknowledgments

One of the pleasures of scholarship is in continually rediscovering the kindness and the generosity of the many people who will give time and take trouble to help the scholar in his task. I am sincerely grateful to all of the people mentioned here for their help in this way.

Grateful acknowledgment is made to William Morrow and Company, Inc., for permission to quote from *Proud Riders And Other Poems*, by H. L. Davis, copyright 1942 by H. L. Davis, and from *Winds of Morning*, by H. L. Davis, copyright 1952 by H. L. Davis.

Quotations from H. L. Davis's journals and correspondence are included through the courtesy of the Humanities Research Center, The University of Texas at Austin, and with the kind permission of Mrs. Elizabeth Thayer Hobson, Mr. Davis's widow. Many people at The University of Texas provided kind, thoughtful, and prompt assistance to my study of the Davis papers there. I am particularly grateful to Mrs. June Moll, formerly librarian of the Humanities Research Library; to Mr. John R. Payne, presently associate librarian there; and to Mr. David Farmer, assistant director of the Humanities Research Center.

Mr. Quentin Davis very kindly helped me distinguish fact from fiction in determining the biographical details for H. L. Davis, and he also helped me gain insight into his brother's personality.

Mr. George B. Abdill, curator of the Douglas County Museum, Roseburg, Oregon, took me to Quentin Davis and spent a warm Oregon summer day showing me the area in which H. L. Davis spent his early childhood. He also gave me access to letters and photographs in the Douglas County Museum.

Mr. Martin Schmitt, Special Collections librarian at the University of Oregon Library, was helpful not only in giving me access to Davis materials in that library, but also in referring me to Mr. Abdill and in conducting a statewide search, unfortunately fruitless, for copies of the *Antelope Herald*.

Mildred Bowen Ingram generously provided a copy of her informal memoir of Davis's time in Tennessee and, in addition, gave me valuable insights into the years of their acquaintance following the Tennessee visit.

Professor Richard W. Etulain of Idaho State University, who has long been a student and bibliographer of Davis, gave me valuable advice and leads to Davis materials, both personally and through his published bibliographies.

Mr. Irving Ascher, of Indian Wells, California, helped me locate some of the scanty material available on Davis's work for motion picture studios in Hollywood. Others who helped me find and gain access to scattered Davis correspondence include Ms. Margaret McFadden, assistant curator for Manuscripts and Archives at the Joseph Regenstein Library, University of Chicago; Mrs. Karyl Winn, curator of Manuscripts, University of Washington Libraries; and Miss Mary Washington Frazer, senior archivist, Tennessee State Library and Archives in Nashville.

Mrs. LaVonne Helmling, Miss Susan Kain, and Mrs. Marcia Lukes have been patient, indefatigable, always cheerful and helpful in typing and assembling the manuscript.

Any household in which a book is being written is likely to have a husband or wife who must endure a spouse's preoccupation with the work. In ours, Genny has not only patiently accepted the demands on my time, and found ways to relieve me of other tasks, but she has also been an indispensable researcher, advisor, reader, sounding board, and source of encouragement. Our daughter, Elaine, and our son, Christopher, have helped examine documents and publications and have been patient, pleasant traveling companions in our search for materials. I hope they like the result.

Chronology

1894   Harold Lenoir Davis born October 18, at Rone's Mill, near Nonpareil, Oregon, to James Alexander and Ruth Bridges Davis. Father a country schoolteacher.

1906 - Family lives in Antelope, Oregon. Summer of 1907, Harold
1908   works for *Antelope Herald*.

1908   Family moves to The Dalles, Oregon.

1912   Harold graduates from high school in The Dalles.

1912 - Deputy county assessor, deputy sheriff, Wasco County,
1916   Oregon.

1917   Survey work for United States General Land Office. Tries to enroll in Stanford University; learns funds insufficient; returns to The Dalles.

1918   Drafted into army in September, serves in Quartermaster Corps, Fort McDowell, California; makes corporal; given clerical duty; discharged in December; returns to The Dalles. Sends group of poems to Harriet Monroe.

1919   "Primapara" poems published in April issue of *Poetry*. Wins Helen Haire Levinson Prize.

1919   Works in or near The Dalles at variety of jobs. Called
1928   leading poet of Northwest by Carl Sandburg.

1920   Ten poems, June issue of *Poetry*.

1925   Seven poems, March issue of *Poetry*.

1926   With James Stevens, publishes *Status Rerum*.

1928   Stories on which Davis collaborated with Stevens, "Occidental's Prodigal," "Oleman Hattie," published in *Adventure*. Stevens listed as author. May 25, marries Marion Lay; moves to Bainbridge Island, Washington.

1929   First prose fiction under own name, "Old Man Isbell's Wife," February issue of *American Mercury*. Four more short prose works published.

1930   Moves to Arizona. "Flying Switch," "Shiloh's Waters," and "A Town in Eastern Oregon" published.

1931   "Extra Gang" and "Team Bells Woke Me" published. Returns to Bainbridge Island, Washington.

1932	Receives Guggenheim Exchange Fellowship to Mexico.
1933	"New Birds," "In Argos" published, ending career as a poet.
1935	First novel, *Honey in the Horn*, published; wins Harper Novel Prize. Begins dispute with Harper.
1936	*Honey in the Horn* wins Pulitzer Prize for 1936.
1937	Moves to Napa, California.
1939	"Open Winter" and "Homestead Orchard" published.
1941	"A Flock of Trouble" published.
1942	*Proud Riders* published by Harper and Brothers.
1943	Harold and Marion Lay Davis divorced.
1947	By this time, probably earlier, Davis writing for motion pictures. Legal dispute with Harper and Brothers settled. Morrow publishes *Harp of a Thousand Strings*.
1949	*Beulah Land* published.
1952	*Winds of Morning* published.
1953	Marries Elizabeth Tonkin Martin del Campo on June 2 in San Antonio, Texas. *Team Bells Woke Me* published.
1953 - 1961	*Holiday* essays published.
1954	"The Elusive Trail to the Old West," critical essay about Western writing.
1956	Left leg amputated in October as result of acute arteriosclerosis.
1957	*The Distant Music* published.
1959	*Kettle of Fire* published.
1960	Dies October 31 in San Antonio after two heart attacks.

CHAPTER 1

The Basic Framework

I Origins and Early Years

H AROLD Lenoir Davis was born at Rone's Mill near Nonpareil
in Douglas County, Oregon, on October 18, 1894.[1] He was the
first of four sons born to James Alexander and Ruth Bridges Davis.
The others were Percy (born 1896, died 1910), Quentin (born 1901),
and Richard (born 1911). James Davis was a country schoolteacher
who was noted for his ability to maintain discipline under the difficult conditions of a one-room country schoolhouse. He had lost a
leg in a sawmill accident when he was only six years old, but he was
active, athletic, the best shot in southern Oregon, and an accomplished horse trainer who also wrote poetry and who read the
better American writers of the time. During his years in The Dalles,
he was also county assessor and sold insurance. In later years,
Harold apparently did not get along well with his father. When
James Davis died on June 1, 1932, Harold was in Mexico and unable, or unwilling, to return during his father's final sickness and for
his burial.

Harold Davis's grandparents on both sides of the family were
from Tennessee. His father's father, Alexander Davis, had been killed fighting for the Confederacy at Champion's Hill in the Vicks-
burg campaign in 1863. Harold in his journal says that his grandfather was a lieutenant in the 38th East Tennessee Infantry.[2]
Davis's step-grandfather Moser, who was sent to tell the widow of
her husband's death, returned to marry her after the war and to
take the family, including the infant James Davis, west to settle in
Oregon.[3] Harold Davis's maternal grandfather was a Hard-shell
Baptist preacher, Daniel Bridges, who migrated from Tennessee to
the Umpqua Valley in Oregon in 1852.[4] Thus on both sides
Harold's family background was Southern and educated, but they
had had recent pioneering experience and followed basically rural
occupations.

An old Tennessee frontier tradition says that a father should teach his son to ride, to shoot, and to tell the truth. Although Harold in his later years was not close to his father, he had in his parent a model who knew guns and horses and was enough of an intellectual to understand the complexities of really telling the truth. Throughout Harold's life, he remained interested in guns and hunting, riding was his favorite recreation, and his whole adult life as a writer was spent in a sustained effort to tell the truth about the life he saw around him while he was growing up. Harold's lifelong interest in riding and marksmanship suggests the continuing influence of his family heritage.

Although there seems to be no evidence that Harold was markedly religious in any formal or conventional sense—he was not a member of any church during his adult life—his references to his grandfather Bridges suggest that his minister grandfather was an influence of some importance in his childhood. That and the moral and religious rectitude generally required of rural schoolteachers like his father in the early years of this century suggest that Harold was reared in a Protestant Christian context that provided a basis for the extensive use of the Christian tradition so evident in his fiction.

In 1896, the year the second son, Percy, was born, James Davis moved his family to Looking Glass, then in 1897 to Drain, and in 1898, following available teaching jobs, to Ten Mile, all in Douglas County, Oregon. Sometime before 1903, the family moved again, this time to Roseburg, and in 1903 to Yoncalla. In 1905, the peripatetic teacher's family moved a few miles to Oakland, Oregon, where Harold spent time in the office of the *Oakland Owl*, the local newspaper. Although Harold later spoke of having worked for that newspaper, his brother Quentin says that the eleven-year-old boy was never actually on the paper's staff. Harold was allowed, however, to practice setting items from the pied type, and some of them were printed.

During these early years of Harold's life, the Davis family lived in the valleys west of the Cascade Mountains, an area of ample moisture, low timbered mountain ridges, and fertile, productive bottomlands. It was a region where the land provided an easy living but no one got rich, where pasture was plentiful for livestock, where game was plentiful for the hunter, and where both winter and summer were mild. In 1906, the whole pattern of their landscape changed when the family moved eastward across the Cascades to the town of Antelope, Oregon. Here in the higher plateau country, where the moist Pacific winds have been wrung dry by the high slopes of the Cascades, the land, the climate, and the life were much different from those of the lush valley of the Umpqua. Here the sagebrush ranches had to be large to carry enough cattle to make a living, and either the farmer ran the gamble of dry-land small grains or he irrigated with water from the mountains. Sheepherders ranged far with their flocks to find enough forage. Here was a harsher country with greater hardship for those who lived in it, but they had wider vistas open to their eyes and, perhaps, their minds.

The Davises lived in Antelope only two years, 1906 to 1908, but Harold's fiction repeatedly shows that the region made a deep impression upon his imagination. Harold actually did not get the wide experience as cowboy and sheepherder that some of his later autobiographical accounts claim, but his writer's eye saw enough of this kind of life to give him the necessary sense of what it was like, and during the summer of 1907 he did gain the experience of working in the newspaper office of the *Antelope Herald*.[5]

The Davises made their last move as a family in 1908 when they went to The Dalles, where James Davis was made principal of the high school and where he later filled various county offices for Wasco County. In this Columbia River town Harold saw other aspects of life in the Pacific Northwest—river boating, railroading, and commerce in a trade center that depended on an agricultural hinterland.

Although Percy Davis, Harold's next-younger brother, died in The Dalles in 1910, Harold never mentioned him in his own biographical accounts; but Percy was closest to Harold in age—only two years younger while Quentin was seven years younger and Richard was not born until 1911. Given the personal reticence Davis was later to display in his poetry, and the fact that in later years Harold most consistently gave Percy's birth year as his own, Percy's death may have affected Harold far more deeply than he ever admitted.

What the family gained in The Dalles was an end to frequent moving from one rural community to another after short-term teaching jobs. Harold's home base was The Dalles for twenty years, and he was graduated from the high school there in 1912. Although he was graduated on schedule at the age of eighteen, he implied in later years that his formal education had been casual and erratic. Certainly the eldest son of the high-school principal would not have found his family's attitude toward his schooling to be casual, although his own attitude toward the formalities of school may have made him what today would be called an "underachiever" so far as grades are concerned. According to his brother Quentin, Harold was in those years, as afterward, a voracious and rapid reader who might borrow a book from the local bookstore and only reach the curb in front of the building before he sat down and read the whole thing. He was also sometimes casual about school attendance, occasionally skipping classes in favor of sitting on a hill behind the town and reading. He read widely and well, and developed a prodigious memory that retained what he had read in detail. During this time, he became acquainted with the classics and perhaps laid the groundwork for transmuting his religious background into the rich mythological context that he later found so useful in his fiction. With books and literary magazines always available in his home, literary horizons must always have been wide for the Davis family.

Apparently the humor so characteristic of most of his writing had also begun to develop by this time. In the high-school yearbook, Davis wrote the Class Prophecy for 1912, perhaps his first published writing outside of newspaper work in Oakland and in Antelope. As evidence of his reputation for humor, Davis is presented in the Class Will as leaving "his ability as a jokesmith" to Gus Weigelt.[6] Davis's reputation for truancy is suggested by the humorous listing of his favorite book, "In School and Out."

Following his graduation, Harold with the help of his father secured a job as deputy county assessor for Wasco County. Since his primary duty was the collection of taxes and since the authority in Wasco County for that chore was placed in the sheriff's office, Harold was also made a deputy sheriff; but, other than in the collection of taxes, he never actually functioned as the law-enforcement officer that in later biographical accounts he implied that he had been. He continued as a tax collector until 1916 or 1917, when he got a job surveying in the Mount Adams area of Washington for the United States General Land Office.

A college education had apparently not been a serious consideration for Davis, since he had taken the "commercial" course in high school; but, in the fall of 1917, having saved fifteen hundred dollars, he went to Palo Alto with the intention of enrolling in Stanford University to study engineering. He later claimed to have been a student at Stanford, but, when he arrived on campus, he discovered that his savings would not be sufficient to finance a college education, so he decided not to enroll, and after a brief visit to California he returned to The Dalles.[7]

II *Beginning with Poetry*

Harold Davis was drafted into the army on September 23, 1918, at The Dalles. He was assigned immediately to the Quartermaster Corps at Fort McDowell, California, made a clerk, given the rank of corporal, and honorably discharged December 10, 1918, at Fort McDowell after less than three months in the service. When he gave various accounts in later years of his military service, he frequently mentioned being in the cavalry and even claimed to have served in the Seventh Cavalry on the Mexican border in pursuit of Pancho Villa; but the files of the National Personnel Records Center in St. Louis show this all to have been romantic fiction.

The real achievement of those three months in the army, of more importance than pursuit of Pancho Villa, was that Davis sent a group of poems to Harriet Monroe for publication in *Poetry*. These poems, collectively called "Primapara," were accepted and appeared in the April 1919 issue of the magazine, publicly launching Davis's career as a writer and winning for him the Helen Haire Levinson Prize for poetry in 1919. From April 1919 through May 1933, Davis published a total of thirty-nine poems and established a modest but solid reputation among American poets and critics as the leading poet of the Pacific Northwest.

From the time of his discharge from the army, in December 1918, to 1928, Davis lived in or near The Dalles, writing poetry slowly but steadily and becoming knowledgeable about the regional literary scene in the Pacific Northwest. Because of his writing he became acquainted with Carl Sandburg, Robinson Jeffers, and such Northwestern literary figures as James Stevens and Richard Wetjens. To earn a living, he worked at a variety of jobs ranging from bank clerk to timekeeper on a railroad track gang.

Typically Davis's acquaintance with the literary scene in the Pacific Northwest marked him as an irreverent outsider rather than a willing participant in the "polite" circles of the regional literary establishment. He made this point forcefully and publicly in 1926 when he and James Stevens wrote and privately published a small booklet that for a time in the region made big waves: *Status Rerum: A Manifesto, Upon the Present Condition of Northwest Literature.* Although only about two hundred copies were printed, at The

Dalles, the little booklet attracted attention by the vigor and bluntness of its attack on regional writers, editors, and teachers of writing, calling some by name and taking to task the writing programs at both the University of Oregon and the University of Washington. It was such heavy invective against such minor figures that Robinson Jeffers, to whom Davis sent a copy, called it a "rather grimly powerful wheel to break butterflies on."[8]

Status Rerum served as a public declaration of Davis's intention to remain independent of the regional literary establishment. After such invective, forgiveness would have been impossible. He had burned his bridges.

III *Moving to Fiction*

The collaboration with James Stevens in the mid-1920s took other forms, also. Two short stories appearing in 1928 in *Adventure* magazine, "Occidental's Prodigal" and "Oleman Hattie," are said by Davis's brother Quentin to have been written by Davis, although they bear Stevens's name in the publication. Stevens was by then an established writer of short stories about the West, and he could command premium fees from such magazines, but Davis was not yet well known. Apparently the arrangement, if there was one, was designed to get the relatively unknown Davis's work more readily into print and perhaps at a better rate of pay.

Other pressures were moving Davis toward the writing of fiction besides this anonymous success in a pulp adventure magazine. H. L. Mencken, having published some of Davis's poetry, was also urging him to try fiction. Although his poetry was obviously not going to earn enough money to relieve him of the necessity for some other source of income, he married Marion Lay, a newspaperwoman who also had ambitions as a writer of fiction, on May 25, 1928. With all hope of literary patronage in Oregon destroyed by *Status Rerum*, Davis was faced with a series of possibilities and with the necessity for making a clear choice in 1928. He could settle into some non-literary line of work and make a living for himself and his wife and forget about serious and concentrated writing, or he could take the plunge into dependence on his writing of fiction for a sufficient income and abandon the variety of jobs he had held during the years since his graduation from high school. As a final nudge, the political group in Wasco County with which James Davis had been allied, and through which he had often been able to help Harold find work, was voted out of office. This change may finally have made a nonliterary future seem as precarious as the life of a professional writer.

Doubtless helped to his decision by Mencken's encouragement, Davis took the plunge. He and his new wife left The Dalles; moved to Winslow, on Bainbridge Island, Washington; and set out to live on the proceeds of his writing. He was never again to live in Oregon for any extended period of time, although most of his best writing is set in this region. Except for a few months with James Stevens while presenting a program on folklore and folk music over Station KEX in Seattle, and except for a job in a planing mill in Westimber, Oregon, early in 1929, his gainful employment for the rest of his life was in some way as a writer.[9]

For the next few years, the finances of the H. L. Davises were precarious, even at times desperate. In 1930 they moved to Arizona, where their finances apparently reached low ebb, and in 1931 they moved back to Washington. *The American Mercury* persistently reported that Davis was working on a book about American folklore during those years, but Davis makes no mention of such a book in his journal or letters of the period; indeed, he denies it in a note in his journal in 1931.[10] This continuing report may have come from Davis's lifelong interest in and use of folk tales and folk songs which he avidly collected for use in his fiction, but he never published a formal collection or study of folk materials. He became an accomplished guitarist and folksinger, and he was reputedly able to sing purely from memory hundreds of folk songs in several languages.

While in Arizona, Davis applied for a Guggenheim Fellowship to go to Spain to work on a long poem. The fellowship was not granted then; but, after he had returned to Washington, the Guggenheim Foundation offered him in 1932 a reduced stipend of two thousand dollars for a year on an exchange fellowship to Mexico. By that time, the acceptance of such a grant required some rearranging of plans, but he did accept it. He and Marion lived at first in Mexico City, but they later moved to Oaxaca, his home for various periods throughout the remainder of his life.

IV   *The Novels*

Once in Mexico, Davis apparently never worked seriously on the long poem which he had originally proposed in his Guggenheim application. For a time, he continued to produce short stories; but he finally began work on the novel that had been in the back of his mind at least since 1930 when he made fragmentary notes about it in his journal. After the Guggenheim grant was finished, Davis remained in Mexico and continued work on the novel, *Honey in the Horn*, which was finally published in 1935 by Harper. The Davises were still in Oaxaca when word came that *Honey* had won the Harper Novel Prize of seventy-five hundred dollars for the best first novel in 1935. With money from the prize, the Davises left Mexico, bought a car, and started for New York.

In Tennessee, they stopped at Horn Springs, a resort near Lebanon, for a swim; and they so enjoyed the pool that they decided to stay overnight and have another swim the following morning. By morning, Marion was ill with what was diagnosed at Vanderbilt Hospital in Nashville as paratyphoid; she remained hospitalized for weeks; and Harold, who remained at Horn Springs, drove the twenty miles to Nashville each day to see her. Since the Horn Springs Hotel was little used except on weekends and since Davis was permitted to visit Marion only very briefly, he had time for undisturbed work on *Beulah Land*, the plot of which begins in Tennessee. When Marion was finally released from the hospital, he brought her back to the hotel for convalescence. Although the hotel closed after Labor Day, the Horn family had become so attached to the Davises that they permitted the visitors to stay through the winter.[11]

They were still at Horn Springs when word came in the spring of 1936 that *Honey in the Horn* had won the Pulitzer Prize. The announcement was the occasion for a party at Horn Springs, which Davis seems to have enjoyed immensely;[12] but, with his often perverse shyness, he refused his publisher's request that he go to New York, at Harpers' expense, to receive the prize. He said he did not want to make himself "a subject for exhibit."[13] Soon after, the Davises left Horn Springs for California; but they first made a detour to Baltimore and New York, thereby completing the journey they had begun the year before.

In California, the Davises bought a small "ranch" north of San Francisco. The property, called "Deer Lick," was on Lokoya Road near Napa. They were there by mid-May 1937. Davis apparently had an early version of *Beulah Land* in hand, but he continued until 1941 to write short stories as a primary source of income. Settled on his own land, an established writer with a Pulitzer Prize, Davis might have been expected to enter into a period of maximum productivity, but such was not the case. He published no more short stories after 1941, with the exception of "Kettle of Fire" near the end of his career; and his next published novel, *Harp of a Thousand Strings*, did not appear until 1947. This period of low production was the result of two major problems that amounted to crises in Davis's life.

One was personal; the other, with a publisher. Never on very solid ground, Davis's marriage with Marion was in serious trouble by this time. Although they had had periods of estrangement as early as 1931, they did not separate for the final time until February 1942. On June 11, 1942, Marion sued Davis for a divorce by mutual agreement; and the suit was ultimately granted. During these same years, Davis was involved in a long-running dispute with his publisher, Harper and Brothers, apparently over royalty payments for *Honey in the Horn;* but the problem later involved the contractual obligations on both sides for Davis's later novels.

The contract for *Honey* apparently gave Harper an option to publish either Davis's next novel or a volume of his poetry. At various times in his journal, Davis refers to an early version of *Beulah Land* which was apparently in the hands of the publisher, but a decision on that manuscript seems to have been delayed pending settlement of the contract dispute. Harper did publish *Proud Riders*, a collection of Davis's poetry, in 1942; but the dispute as to whether or not the publisher still had an option on Davis's next novel apparently continued. Davis finally referred his side of the matter to an attorney and preparations were made for legal action; but, in June 1947, the matter was settled out of court. In the meantime, Davis had become friends with Thayer Hobson, editor-in-chief at William Morrow, who had expressed interest in publishing Davis's work. One of the results of the settlement with Harper was, therefore, that all rights to Davis's writing were assigned to William Morrow and Company.

With marital and legal problems solved, Davis began a period of much greater productivity that in the next ten years resulted in four novels, a collection of his earlier short stories, a book of essays, and a number of shorter pieces and movie-script projects. *Harp of a Thousand Strings* was published almost immediately by Morrow in 1947, and *Beulah Land* followed in 1949. Although Davis had been working on *Beulah Land* earlier, he finished the published version after he had completed *Harp*.[14]

The early 1940s were a time of severe financial difficulty that eas-
ed considerably later in the decade. Besides the resumption of novel
publication in the late 1940s, Davis by 1947 was working as a writer—or rewriter—for various motion-picture studios in Hollywood.[15] These assignments came at intervals through 1954, when he
worked for Paramount on a script for Emerson Hough's *Covered
Wagon*. Some of this work may have been background research
rather than writing. Unfortunately, Davis was troubled during those
years by occasional illnesses that apparently involved heart
problems.[16]

Davis's friendship with the Western poet Thomas Hornsby Ferril,
which began in 1939, provided interesting sidelights on the years of
renewed productivity. In the pages of the *Rocky Mountain Herald*,
a weekly newspaper edited and published by Ferril and his wife,
Ferril began mentioning Davis and his work; and, as Davis's novels
were published, Ferril's newspaper gave them sympathetic reviews.
Beginning at least by 1942, and lasting until 1955, Davis contributed letters, short essays, and tall tales to the *Herald*. For a
number of those years, Davis was actually listed on the masthead of
the paper as a correspondent, although it is doubtful that he was
ever paid.[17] These pieces, mostly of an ephemeral nature, range in
topic from Shakespeare's sonnets to Spanish names to current
events. Only one, the tall tale "The Electric Bulldog" (May 12,
1945), seems likely to survive.

Davis's fourth novel, *Winds of Morning*, was published in 1952
with good reviews and with selection by the Book-of-the-Month
Club. In terms of critical reception, this book was the third high
point of Davis's career. This success was followed the next year by a
collection of his short stories, *Team Bells Woke Me*, which also
received good reviews. Davis's career was clearly back on the track,
and he was again achieving critical recognition.

On June 2, 1953, in San Antonio, Texas, Davis married Elizabeth
Tonkin Martin del Campo. The marriage was a happy one, and the
couple spent the next four years alternating between Mexico and
California. Davis was at work on film assignments, travel essays for
Holiday magazine, and his next novel, *The Distant Music*. But
Davis's health again became a problem. He had had difficulty for
years with circulation in his legs, and at times he had to go to bed
and apply heat for relief from the pain. The trouble had begun as
early as 1925, and he had been hospitalized by it in 1950 in Santa
Monica.[18] Finally, as a result of acute arteriosclerosis, his left leg

was amputated in October, 1956, at a hospital in Mexico.[19] Although he forced himself to continue to write and to read, he was never without pain for any substantial period of time for the remaining four years of his life. His physicians did not expect him long to survive the operation, but he did. When he finally left the hospital, he was adjusted to the loss of his limb (reminding himself that his father had made such an adjustment) and was determined to keep working.

Davis never really recovered from the amputation. After six months in the hospital, he was able to return to his home and to write; but his work was the result of courage and endurance and ability to concentrate in spite of pain. He continued to read widely, and he continued to write the series of travel essays for *Holiday* that he had begun in 1953. He produced seven more essays after returning from the hospital; wrote one last short story, "Kettle of Fire"; saw the collection of essays and the short story through the press as *Kettle of Fire* (1959); saw his last novel, *The Distant Music* (1957), through the press; and began work on another novel, tentatively called "Exit, Pursued by a Bear."

Photographs of Davis toward the end of his life show a man who looked far younger than his actual age. Indeed, in Davis's journals and letters there is never a sense of twilight, of looking back on a life nearly spent. The late essays he wrote for *Holiday* do indeed recall past experiences and times that have changed, but even in them there is little of the golden note of nostalgia. Instead, the tone is one of a man with an important life still left to live, but he remembers what he has already lived with a savor he expects to continue to have for experience.

Entries in Davis's journal during those final years reflect the pain and his impatience with his illness, but they are never the entries of a man who has stopped living, reading, and thinking. The last entry deals with his reading of Catullus, Vergil, Horace, and Ovid.

On October 18, 1960, during a visit to San Antonio, Davis suffered a heart attack and was hospitalized. On October 31, he suffered a second attack, which was fatal.

V Sorting Biographical Fact and Fiction

Such are the basic biographical facts of H. L. Davis's life, sorted and verified from a welter of misinformation fabricated for the most part by Davis himself and perpetuated by incautious scholars and

critics who have overlooked the inconsistencies and accepted
Davis's word. The reasons behind Davis's fabrication of a varied
past remain to be resolved by a biographer, but a few likely
possibilities readily present themselves. As has already been
suggested, his adoption of the birth date of his brother Percy, who
died in adolescence, coupled with his later reticence about the existence of that brother, suggest deep emotional involvement, but
definitive judgment of this situation would require extensive in-
vestigation, if indeed any judgment were ever possible.

On the other hand, there are more direct and obvious reasons for
much of Davis's concoction of a romantic past that included cow-
punching, sheepherding, and pursuing Pancho Villa. When Davis
began his literary career in 1919 at the age of twenty five, the new
poetry was established and accepted at least by literary intellec-
tuals; and the "lost generation" of young writers returned from the
Great War and the young expatriates living in Paris were to come to
the literary forefront in the next few years. Much of the attention of
critics was turned to the young, the new, the dashing, the romantic;
the excitement of the Roaring Twenties was beginning to appear. In
such a context, a high-school principal's oldest son, who had hardly
traveled out of his native state, who had worked at nothing more exciting than being a county tax collector, and whose military experience was nothing more dashing than being drafted into a
clerkship in the neighboring state of California for less than three
months might well feel that his career would be helped by the addition of a little romantic imagination to the biographical facts. Many
another creative artist has done as much.

Then, as well as now, image could play an important role in the
fortunes of a young poet trying to gain recognition, and some of the
early critical comment on Davis's poetry and short prose suggests
that a little trumped-up romance may indeed have helped. Readers
are often attracted to works that they believe to be based on actual
experience. Although Davis had not had the broad and colorful experience that he claimed, it is obvious now that he had the writer's
imaginative sensitivity that made the slightest peripheral contact
with a way of life enough to make that life available to his fiction.
Two weeks of herding sheep for a friend, a summer working on a
little newspaper in a sagebrush town—such brief experiences were
enough to give Davis the base of experience he needed. He was, as
Henry James urged writers to be, one of those on whom nothing

was lost. If he had fully lived the lives about which he wrote, he would have had no time for his art. His work represents not a telling of tales from his colorful experiences but a major achievement of the literary imagination. With his career completed and his work published and ready to stand on its own merits as an important part of the literature of America, the time has arrived to set the record straight.

CHAPTER 2

The Poetry

LITTLE critical attention has been paid to the poetry of H. L. Davis since the early 1930s, when he abandoned writing poems for fiction. Indeed, some critics who value his novels and short stories seem unaware that he has written a substantial body of poetry. Yet for his first ten years as a writer, approximately from 1918 to 1928, he was primarily a poet. This period not only produced work deserving critical attention, but also undoubtedly had an important influence on his development as a novelist.

I The "Primapara" Poems

Davis's debut as a poet could hardly have been more encouraging. While he was still in the army in the autumn of 1918, he sent a group of poems to Harriet Monroe for publication in *Poetry*. Their arrival in Chicago created a stir in the magazine's editorial office, where Davis was hailed as a major new poet: "Their long lines and slow rhythms sounded a new music, a strain original and noble."[1] When Mrs. Monroe published this group of eleven poems under Davis's general title, "Primapara," in the April 1919 issue, she gave his poems the lead position in the magazine. Because of her enthusiasm, she continued to show the poems to writers and critics in Chicago and New York, and to praise them as the work of a new Western poet who wrote about the common people and the Western landscape. Through her efforts, Davis very quickly became known as a promising young writer from whom great things might be expected.

Davis himself seems to have been surprised by such a reception for his first offerings. In his letter of response to Mrs. Monroe, he wrote, "I was surprised to learn that you have found the poems of such merit. . . . There seems something suspicious about their turning out so well. . . ."[2] Suspicious or not, publication of this first group of poems immediately brought a letter of praise from Carl Sandburg and, perhaps at Sandburg's urging, an inquiry from Holt and Company about publishing a volume of Davis's work.[3] In 1920, the *Poetry* staff backed its judgment by awarding the "Primapara" poems the Helen Haire Levinson Prize for 1919.

The order in which the eleven "Primapara" poems were published offered no clear thematic structure from one poem to the next. They apparently were grouped under this name simply because they were the first poems submitted and not because they had any relationship with one another. Indeed, in *Proud Riders And Other Poems*, a selected collection published by Harper and Brothers in 1942, these poems are scattered throughout the volume.

"The Sweet Tasting" (renamed "Proud Riders" in the later book),[4] the first poem in the group, is spoken by cattle drivers who, full of the action and energy of fall roundup, are self-consciously aware of the watching farmers and townspeople. Although youth is not mentioned, it is a youthful poem that glorifies the action and the vigor of the cattle drive, and that makes endurance of the harsh wind and cold a part of the pride of the riders. At the same time, curiously yet successfully, it is an autumnal poem that is about the end of the season, not a beginning. A youthful assertion of life in a dying season, this poem is a statement of internal fire when the yellow leaves are falling into the black waters of death.

The second poem, "Running Vines in a Field,"[5] is spoken from outside the group rather than by a participant. Like many of Walt Whitman's poems, Davis's is addressed to its subject, "You loose haired women in the field." To them the speaker promises, "I shall be half among your hearts with speech." The young speaks to the old; the sexual ("It is love with me") speaks to those made sexless by age ("Since you are too old for love you make a garden"); and Davis introduces the metaphorical parallel between sexual love and the cultivation of the land and cycle of the seasons that he uses frequently. As in "Proud Riders," the setting and tone are autumnal ("the red leaves of the blackberry vines / Are hoar with frosty dew"), and the dying season is confronted by an affirmation of youth. But since the youth carries the scars of experience—"Love and my sorrow, the disastrous passages"—the poem fails to become an affirmative one, for even the tempered assertion of the youth finally does not avail. The old women at last, in spite of the speech of the youth "half among their hearts," forget the speaker "for a little pride of old time." The autumnal tone prevails, and there is only memory as the lives of the women move through the autumnal "putting by" into the death of winter.

In "A Field by the River,"[6] the speaker is again an outsider, an observer, who is even further removed now because there is no suggestion of interaction. The speaker is watching women walk through their own autumnal fields and beyond them into un-cultivated ground beside a river. In this poem, the sexual imagery grows more complex, more obscure, and more essential to the meaning. The white river bird of the first line, which is associated through color imagery with the white dresses of the women and with "the white stubble of their own field's / Edge," links the whiteness (the presence of all visual colors, thus complete ex-perience) with wildness, sexuality, and the sources of life. Within the same pattern, the wind "Comes like a bird from the river, and blows their dresses." The river, the source of the "white river-bird" and of the birdlike wind, is the source of wildness, of the spring flood that has set the margin to the cultivation of the land, the line beyond which "the reaper / Has never been driven." This edge of cultivation is the limit of the women's safe, ordered existence, the limit up to which their relationship with the sources of life is under their control.

In the autumn, after the harvest, the women cross the forbidden boundary: "among the willows and high cold weeds / Where the flood bred pale snapdragons in the shade." They go where, in the spring, "the water felt at the young grain," because now that it is autumn they have nothing to fear from the wildness of the river and the river bird, and so "At the flood margin which they feared their pleasure is." The flight of the white bird reminds them of the margin they have crossed, but "two seasons / Are to come before Spring comes." Without fear, they can venture into the wildness in the season of dying, but not in the season of birth, not in the floods of spring.

The poetic form of these first three short poems is a free-verse ap-proximation of blank verse. All are unrhymed. Many lines of each are clearly iambic pentameter, but other lines must be distorted to force them into pentameter, and in those lines the iamb disappears entirely. The lines are consistently long and loosely constructed. Their quiet tone, achieved both through the diction and through the absence of any distinct or regular rhythmic pattern, suggests either quiet conversation or pensive soliloquy.

"In the Field,"[7] the fourth of the "Primapara" group, is more nearly regular in scansion, and might be regarded as blank verse, but in each of the three stanzas there is a single, casual rhyme. The placement of these rhymes, however, is so random that they are hardly perceived by the reader. "In the Field" is a retrospective love poem that recounts the speaker's time with a beautiful "alien" girl: "I wonder at you moreover because of your people, / Whose daughters should not seem sweet. . . ." The remembrance, however, is of things past, because the remembered "green shining meadow" early in the poem gives way to the girl working with her people in fields "where about cold low springs the smoke / From waters at morning stains the cold air all day." As with the preceding poems in the group, the effect is quietly pensive, and there is little sense of structural pattern.

The next poem of the group, "The Gypsy Girl,"[8] is similar in form and tone to "In the Field," except that the random, unobtrusive rhymes occur more frequently; but they still have little impact on the reader's sense of the structure of the poem.

Again in autumn, "The Gypsy Girl" recounts offers made by an already pregnant gypsy girl to the speaker of the poem, who mourns for a lost love and refuses the gypsy's advances. Here the sexual imagery that is explicitly associated with gardening, harvest, and the cycle of the seasons is achieved with a line that occurs three times: "what is not picked now in the garden will never be picked." The connection of the garden imagery with the pregnant girl is made specific in the paralleling of colors between the first and second stanzas. In the first stanza, the colors of the autumn garden are presented: yellow cherry leaves, brown weed seeds, gray stems and seeds, dusty grass, and, in an image, pale green water. At the end of the stanza, the girl appears with yellow face and black hair. Because her colors are also yellow and pale green, with red in the place of brown and with silver in place of gray, the poet makes her more vivid than the garden, or perhaps more garish.

Coming through willows, with her yellow face above the green water, her personification of the autumnal garden is made explicit by her dress, "stretched with her young one / So that its pattern shaped into big ungodly flowers." By this developing connection in imagery between the garden and the people in it, the seasons of the garden become the seasons of life. Thus the refrain, "what is not picked now in the garden will never be picked," becomes a renunciation of love.

"The Spirit,"[9] one of Davis's most difficult poems, is also one of his few spring poems; but it is a spring that comes after lost love. Love is replaced by the feminine spirit of spring, who is purely veg-etative ("I half live, like a stalk") and is not a real girl ("but no girl orders me"). The spirit then becomes the sublimated one of spring in nature without the explicit sexual involvement of a real girl—a spirit for a heart which now "owns no favor or love." The form is free verse with neither rhyme nor regular patterns of scansion.

"My Step-Grandfather"[10] is one of Davis's most straightforward poems in content; and, of the "Primapara" group, it is the most regular in form. It presents an old man and a boy, resting at noon from their farm work. The old man is remembering the Civil War and his service under Robert E. Lee—his loyalty and his pride at serving under such a man, even in a losing cause. The boy's response is that he, too, could follow what he loved and "go hungry and in great shame, and, for a cause, be proud." This poem is much clearer and more explicit. Drawn apparently much more directly from Davis's own experience, it presents that experience much more openly. His step-grandfather fought with the Confederate Army and did not remain in the South after the war. Like the biblical Queen Esther, who is compared to the old man in the poem, Davis's family was an emigrant one that still felt loyalties to its ancestral home and people.

The lines of "My Step-Grandfather" remain long, loosely con-structed, basically iambic pentameter, but the rhymes are much more frequent and play a clearer role in the effect of the poem. Even here, however, there is no regular rhyming pattern to the lines; they range from full rhyme (*spell-fell, vines-pines,* for exam-ple) through partial rhymes such as *pines-times* and *frost-most* to such near rhymes as *women-trimming.* Unlike any other poem in this group, every line ends with at least a near rhyme with some other line. This interesting early association between explicit specificity in subject matter and regularity of form suggests that Davis had tighter, more conscious control of poetic form when his subject permitted more direct statement.

"Oakland Pier,"[11] too, seems drawn directly from Davis's own ex-perience, from his time in the army. This poem presents the thoughts and conversations of soldiers about to be discharged, con-trasted with the memories of a veteran professional soldier who is waiting with them on the pier. In "Oakland Pier," however, the in-direction and the free-verse format are resumed, just as they are in "The Old Are Sleepy,"[12] which is a difficult poem filled with indirection and ambiguity. In a reversal of the pattern of those poems in which youth is the apparent subject, only to end with reminders of mortality, this poem seems at first to be about the old named in the title, but it concludes with "a distant spring's beauty" with a "mouth of music." The beauty could only be that of the spring flowing between the wheat fields were it not for the pervasive sexual imagery of the poem (even the old men "have put the hills in foal"). Adding to the complexity of the poem is not only the unidentified speaker but also the unidentified "you" to whom the poem is apparently spoken. These two personages bear some apparent but undefined relationship to the "they," the old men and their women. The last line suggests that the "you" corresponds with the women who lie by the old men who have "put the hills in foal." And yet, as they await the harvest, the old men sleep with a pride in the beauty, a pride to be wept for, because the beauty has been changed, or will change.

If we return, then, to the sexual implications of the imagery, we can begin to understand the complex, indirect pattern of meaning. On the one hand, we have the phallic implications of the straight stalks of wheat, "straight weeds" where the men walk, and slim, vertical poplars. These are all associated with dryness, dust, and wind in a season no longer needing moisture for fertility. Contrasted with these are the soft hills, which are "in foal" and which seem associated with the women "who lie uneasy at night" with the contented old men.

Nestled among these hills is a spring, associated with a series of yonic images: the spring itself; the bending, submissive willows in contrast with the erect poplars; the "mouth of music"; the "low hair"; and the "beauty in which music is." This sexual association is made more explicit by referring to the "distant spring's beauty" as "her of whom you are proud." The speaker of the poem in the final stanza spends a night with the "distant spring's beauty," feeling "her mouth and low hair." Strangely, the outcome of this is not joy but sadness. The rain that in an earlier season brought forth the growth on the "hills in foal" will darken the willows of the spring and lead the women to cry for the pride of the old men in the distant spring's beauty. The coming of the fertilizing rain represents a loss of beauty and of basis for pride. Thus what appears to be an erotic poem closes with a lament for lost virginity, and for innocence lost inevitably in the cycle of the seasons of life.

"Flags,"[13] which begins with delight in irises (flags) in bloom, leads through a reverie of the wild flowers of the speaker's home country, but ends with a Whitmanesque apostrophe, "Play up a tune, sing loud and handsome, O soul!" Unlike love, the garden abides. Interesting in the closing lines of this poem is the first reference in Davis's writing to the folk song about honey in the horn, from which the title for his first novel came. The same figure, honey in the horn, opens "The Valley Harvest,"[14] the last poem of the "Primapara" group. It is an image of plenty, of bountiful harvest that the women call for and urge on the men. Again, the speaker in the poem is the outsider; an itinerant leading his horse from the spring, he is ignored by the women, who speak only to the men mowing in their harvest. The outsider is left with an image of loneliness: "What is by the spring? A bird, and a few old leaves."

Of the "Primapara" group, only the last two poems were not reprinted when, in the late 1930s, Davis assembled *Proud Riders And Other Poems*. Six of the eleven were immediately anthologized by Alfred Kreymborg in *Others for 1919: An Anthology of New Verse* (1920). Kreymborg called Davis the least bookish of the far-West poets; he thought him original and not rhetorical.[15]

The major themes and techniques of most of Davis's poetry occur in this first group: the vividly realized landscape peopled by hazy, ephemeral characters; the indirection to the point of reticence; the frequently autumnal tone coupled with a system of basically sexual images operating from the cycle of the seasons, of planting and harvest. The long, loose lines and the occasional cataloging of features of the landscape, of people, and of occupations, all from the central vantage point of the persona who speaks for the poet, suggest the influence of Whitman; but Davis's lines are tighter than Whitman's, and he does not often approach Whitman's vigor and enthusiasm. He is more often reflective, retrospective, and melancholy. The form generally is free verse that approximates blank verse. When rhymes occur, they are random and unobtrusive.

These promising first poems, Davis later said, were in imitation of the shorter poems of the German poet Detlev von Liliencron (1844 - 1908).[16] If such imitation did play a role in Davis's first poems, it was in spirit and approach more than in subject matter or technique. In their ironic view of death, their consciousness of man as an ephemeral event on the eternal face of nature, and their Naturalism flowing into Impressionism, Davis and Liliencron have areas of common ground. The same themes, however, recur consistently in Davis's prose as well as in his poetry, suggesting that, in Liliencron,

Davis found not a model but rather a kindred view of similar subjects.

Perhaps the real significance of Davis's mention of Liliencron lies in its demonstration that Davis was widely read and that even his earliest published poetry is not folk art written by an unlettered cowboy from the ranges of the Pacific Northwest, but sophisticated work by a man who was writing consciously from a rich literary heritage. Perhaps Harriet Monroe was correct in characterizing Davis as "a pastoral poet of the great western ranges,"[17] but he had the same depth of cultural background as those American poets not born so far west.

II *The Major Poetic Production*

Davis followed this initial success with nine poems in the June 1920 issue of *Poetry* and with two more in the October 1922 issue. Again the tone is generally autumnal and retrospective, and frequent references are made to a woman now dead and sadly remembered. In "The Rain Crow,"[18] one of Davis's best, the subject is a friend who "knew so much, and not that she would die!" The poem shows that something even so common as death is a new wonder when it takes one we know. "The Market Gardens"[19] mourns the death of a woman "whose love / I could not have, and grieved for." In the Spoon River manner, "October: 'The Old Eyes' "[20] arrives at insight through the ghost of Eusebia Owen, who returned in the cold October wind to show the desolation behind the apparent contentedness of her life, to show the poet that "we were less friends than ever I had dreamed." "Dog Fennel"[21] laments a dead sister, again in an autumnal setting. Whether it is an older woman or a "dead sister" (Davis never had a sister), the focus in these and in many other of Davis's poems is on women. Also in this group, although it does not lament a death, is "In This Wet Orchard,"[22] which recalls an early desire for an older woman and thus evokes a memory of a spirit of youthful joy.

Only in "The Threshing Floor" and in "To the River Beach" do we find frank joy in life in this group. In "The Threshing Floor,"[23] however, the speaker in the poem is again the outsider, watching from a distance and remembering men less simple than the threshers. Even "To the River Beach"[24] is a savoring of life in the autumn, a last taste of the fruits of the season past. Most notably in "Open Hands,"[25] this group of poems has the same reticence, or blurring of focus, that makes some of the "Primapara" poems so difficult.

Davis did not publish again until 1925, when seven poems appeared in the March issue of *Poetry* (290 - 300). These themes are again much the same. Three poems recollect a mother figure—"Mid-September,"[26] "Renewing Windbreak,"[27] and "The Deep Water"[28]—and the landscape continues to play a dominant role in all seven poems. In "The River People,"[29] the poet deals directly with the effect of the landscape on the nature of the people who live in it. "Binding Hands" begins as a man's reminiscent bequeathing of the landscape to children, but it ends with a cryptic suggestion of sexual love. As before, an autumnal awareness of mortality dominates all of these poems and the lines are long, arhythmic free verse.

When *American Mercury* published Davis's next work, "Of the Dead of a Forsaken Country," in its November 1926 issue,[30] the poem was his first to appear outside the pages of *Poetry*. An excellent representative of Davis's mature poetic style, the poem deals directly with themes and environments that were to run through much of his fiction: the abandoned and deteriorating homestead; the receding of human life from the land after the tumult, dreams, work, and suffering of the pioneers; a pastoral illustration of the vanity of human wishes. The poem offers neither resolution nor escape; it merely presents the eternal landscape and the ephemeral humanity ebbing and flowing across it. All is seen in retrospective dimness, and the speaker is recollecting courage and suffering and loss that have left only abandoned houses and dying orchards. Often in his prose Davis's central character finds himself in a forsaken country trying to learn the lesson such a land can teach about the varying tides of human fortune. This poem is an early, and preliminary, exploration of that theme.

Even though "White Petal Nanitch," published in the January 1927 issue of *Poetry*,[31] is set in the springtime and ends with the words of the youngest man, it concludes with the confrontation of death, not life.[32] Paradoxically, at the loss of the petals of spring and with the onset of fruition, at the end of plowing and in the time of planting, Davis gives us from the mouth of the youngest man in the group, the representative of youth, a statement of the mortality—even the willing and accepting mortality—of our flesh. Out of the season of beginnings from which the Christian tradition builds symbols of immortality, Davis gives us a *memento mori*.

III   *Narrative Transition*

In the late 1920s Davis began experimenting with other forms and line lengths, as illustrated by three poems he published in the September 1928 issue of *Poetry*. Davis, who was interested in and very knowledgeable about folk songs, presented in "Steel Gang"[33] a narrative about track-building on the railroad. Unlike his usual free verse, "Steel Gang" was written in couplets of iambic heptameter and with the style and diction of a folk ballad. He drew again from railroading for "Cloudy Day,"[34] but this lyric has short lines and an irregular but significant rhyming pattern. Then in "Rivers to Children"[35] he returns to the *ubi sunt* theme, still with short lines and irregular rhymes. It is difficult to guess where these new forms and styles might have led in poetry because Davis had turned his attention to writing short stories by 1928. After that year, he published only five more poems.

"Crop Campers," published in the January 1929 issue of *American Mercury*,[36] a narrative written in a loose approximation of blank verse, is another twilight-retrospective poem about a kind of people and a way of life in the rural Northwest, and is told through the voice of a woman. "Threshing Crew Woman," [37] published in a 1930 compendium of folk tales, is a "folk" ballad in rhymed couplets of iambic tetrameter. In "Juan Chacon,"[38] also published in 1930, Davis returned to his earlier style and forms to examine the fate of pioneer leaders who, after settlement, are no longer needed by their people. Davis had explored this theme ten years before in "October: 'The Old Eyes,' " and he presented it again in his short story "Old Man Isbell's Wife" in 1929. Before 1929, his chief use of the past either had been introspective for his persona or had been stated in terms of the landscape and the abandoned homesteads and other conventionally romantic reminders of the ephemeral nature of youth and life. In this work, he confronts the past in the individual human terms of Jesse Applegate, an actual pioneer leader; but the poet's third-person stance permits greater objectivity. This increased objectivity is a significant step in Davis's maturing as a literary artist.

The two poems Davis published in *Poetry* in 1933, his last to be presented in a periodical, might be said to represent the alpha and omega of his poetry. In "New Birds,"[39] he returns again to the long, unrhymed line, to the focus on nature, and to a final stanza that makes an oblique reference to a love that he expects to lose. In this case, the final stanza seems tacked on as an afterthought and weakens the poem. Thus, though it comes late, "New Birds" does not offer a strong example of Davis's early style. "In Argos,"[40] on the other hand, is technically the best of his rhymed narrative poems. It is a first-person narrative by a clearly established persona not associated with the poet. The artistic maturity and dramatic sophistication of this work suggest that, had he continued to write poetry, he might have produced some very significant work in this form. Instead, of course, his development as a writer was moving toward prose fiction, an equally logical transition at this point. His poetry, which served as an apprenticeship, led finally through the short story to the novel, the major form for which Davis is known.

After 1933, Davis published no poetry other than his volume of selected poems, *Proud Riders And Other Poems*, in 1942. This volume was ready some years before, and it did not represent a renewed interest or a further development on Davis's part after nearly a decade of writing fiction. The volume is poorly produced: it has several typographical errors, and one poem, "A Hill Come Out of the Sea," is printed under its own title and then elsewhere under the title "After Love," which does not fit the content of the poem. I have been unable to discover a poem under this second title in Davis's published work; but since he did alter some titles in *Proud Riders*, this title may have been intended as a renaming of an already-published poem. Of those published works not already included in the volume, "Open Hands" would appear to fit the "After Love" title most closely; but I have no evidence that would resolve the question.

On the other hand, the title may have represented a previously unpublished poem. Three of the thirty-seven poems in this volume had not been published before—"Mountain Autumns,"[41] "The Deaf and Dumb Girl,"[42] and "Brynhild"[43]—and the others had all appeared in *Poetry* or in *American Mercury*. The new poems do not present either new directions or new development in Davis's poetry. "The Deaf and Dumb Girl" is a narrative rhymed in couplets in the folk manner; "Brynhild" is a lyric with short lines rhyming alternately; and "Mountain Autumns" is a brief poem in the long, quiet lines common to most of Davis's early work.

Poems in the volume are divided into two groups: "Far Western Pastorals" and "Narrative Poems." The division seems arbitrary, even capricious, particularly in the section of narratives. Several poems in this section, including "Cloudy Day," "Proud Riders,"

"Rivers to Children," and "Brynhild," could hardly be considered narratives and seem to have been included in this section only to give balance to the volume.

IV *The Poetic Achievement*

Although there may have been some uncritically romantic response to Davis's poetry as coming from the "Great West," the critical reception of Davis's work remained both favorable and perceptive throughout his years as a practicing poet. Carl Sandburg said in 1927 that Davis was the "only" poet in the Pacific Northwest,[44] and Robinson Jeffers stated that he knew of no other modern poetry through which the countryside appears with such "Virgilian sweetness."[45] Davis's lack of fashionable concern for current ideas, Jeffers concluded, had kept his poetry from receiving wider recognition, but he felt that this characteristic of his poetry would finally make it more durable.

The landscape, however, does not represent the heart of Davis's poems. He uses the land as it responds to the cycles of the seasons, and as it shapes and responds to the people who gain their living from it, as a basic metaphor for human experience and perception. The poetry finally deals with an internal landscape of the poet himself. By looking again through the eye of the imagination at the people and their land and their ways, the poet both praises them (naming the people and the things on the land was to Davis in itself a form of praise) and sets them in order to declare their meaning.[46] Poetry, Davis felt, can be more a way of feeling than a way of saying; it can be something "to which speech is only incidental"; it can be emotion that carries experience "to its end in understanding."[47] Thus Davis is not basically a poet of the West, although he uses the West in his poetry. In fact, he is not the poet of any particular physical locale. Through an emotional intensity of imagination, he gives us an internal landscape available to human experience in any time and place. He gives us not the world, nor the world as he sees it, but how the world affects the internal landscape of a sensitive and sympathetic participant in humanity. If a central theme runs through all of the poetry, it is a love of humanity and a sense of the tragedy of the human condition.

Yet from this very use of the landscape of his imagination, with its symbolic cycles of planting and harvest, river hills and salt sea spray, there is an indistinctness, a blurring of focus, as if in the prevailingly autumnal air our view of the people and the land were partially obscured by the smoke of autumn fires or by the haze of Indian summer. Jeffers called this failure of clarity reticence, but he could not assign a reason to it. He observed that Davis had a keen, virile, decisive mind and that, "if more of that cavalry-captain decisiveness were in the poetry[,] . . . one wouldn't wonder whether haughtiness or evasion blurs the composition a little."[48]

From the broader perspective of Davis's career not only as a poet but also as a writer of short stories and novels, the problem seems more likely to have been associated with a question of esthetic distance between the writer and the subject. If love and sympathy are indeed the central emotions, a lack of esthetic distance could result in a proud reticence and indirection. Davis was reared in a family that was culturally Southern and that would have been taught reticence concerning the deeper emotions. In addition, the masculine tradition of the West, which was suspicious of any kind of serious poetry from a man, also emphasized concealment rather than revelation of emotion. For a man to show emotion was considered weakness, an embarrassment, particularly among those who lived the harshest, most dangerous lives. From this cultural context, "confessional" poetry would have been difficult if not impossible for him; and an examination of Davis's journal helps establish this point. His immediate personal life never appears directly in his writing, even during his times of great personal stress.

Since Davis's landscapes are internal, he is seeking some form of negative capability by which he can remove himself, as poet, from the poem. He uses a variety of devices in attempting to achieve this: chronological distance through remembrance of past times in such poems as "Of the Dead of a Forsaken Country," social distance by making the speaker of the poem an outside observer as in "A Field by the River," and personal distance in identity by creating a specific persona as first-person narrator as in "Crop Campers" and "In Argos." But these techniques do not always serve; and, even when they do, Davis sometimes seems to want more distancing than they can provide. This need leads to the retrospective, indirect quality of many of the poems and to opaquely elliptical language in most. Both characteristics give the reader a sense of evasion and reticence. The ironic humor that serves Davis so well to gain esthetic distance in his fiction does not appear in his poetry except fleetingly in the last line of "Steel Gang."

Another factor that perhaps contributed to the problem was

Davis's own complex view of life. Although he wrote about man from love and sympathy, he saw the weakness, foolishness, and evil in humanity as well as the strength, courage, and love. The ironic humor of his fiction provided a vehicle for expressing this complexity fully, but Davis never developed as satisfactory a technique in his poetry. His closest approach was in "Gypsy Girl," "Crop Campers," "White Petal Nanitch," and "Steel Gang."

Without the freedom such distancing devices could give Davis, he is limited in his imaginative treatment of his material, even though he put supreme artistic value on the imagination: "It is worth less to repeat what men say than to show what they are; and if a man's writing is worth anything, his imagination is worth more—the last thing and maybe the only thing that is new, and that we can take his word for."[49] This statement is significant because Davis regards poetry as an intensely human activity; the poet cannot be the fully detached and disinterested observer of the human scene, but must instead be fully involved in it.[50]

If, as Davis said, poetry is a way through the emotions to the understanding of experience, the difficulty lay in taking the poem through to that understanding on terms available to the reader. Indirection, evasion, reticence erect no barriers to the poet's own understanding because he knows, for example, when an ambiguity offers all of its possible meanings as part of the poem and when only certain choices will serve. The reader, on the other hand, must determine the range and function of a given ambiguity from within the poem. With a consciously reticent poet, the poem is the one place that will not provide the needed information. Providing this information within the poem, yet maintaining his own distance, was Davis's most difficult artistic problem. Until he developed the ironic humor of his prose, he did not have a reliable solution.

Toward the end of his life, Davis made light of his poetry when he wrote in his journal that his poems "never were much,"[51] but he underrated his achievement. In a little more than a decade of writing, Davis produced a body of poetry that was original, characteristic, and of artistic substance. That he did not consistently solve his artistic problems in his poetry may more likely be ascribed to the fact that he moved away from them toward the problems presented by fiction, where he did find solutions. Within this slim body of poetry, Davis has succeeded in creating a landscape that relates both to the actual landscape of his time and place in Oregon and to the inner landscape of the experience and perception of the poet himself. He has peopled this landscape with figures that are not always seen clearly, but that always have a reality and a dignity which relate them to the human experience of any time and place.

For these poems, Davis's long line and his quiet, common, and sometimes slangy language admirably suit the pastoral tone of most of his work. Perhaps his most significant achievement lies in this taking of the ordinary and making it into poetry. Without any of the mannered posing of the self-consciously proletarian poets, Davis presents ordinary people—farmers, track workers, immigrant laborers, cattle drovers, sheepherders—on the land doing their ordinary work. He resorts neither to verbal pyrotechnics nor to extraordinary circumstances to give their lives significance. He simply assumes their significance and so shows them to us that we accept that assumption. In this sense, his is a realistic Western poetry that does not rely on the traditionally picturesque and romantic elements generally associated with "Western" literature.

Davis's poetry deserves critical attention because he developed a distinctive poetic voice to express a body of experience that is both characteristic of a special time and place, and representative of universal human experience. In addition, it deserves attention as the literary apprenticeship of a significant American writer of fiction. Although the ironic boisterousness of much of Davis's fiction cannot be found in his poetry, we can nevertheless see his major themes already beginning to develop, and also the artistic significance of his ironic humor in achieving esthetic distance from his material.

Much of his prose style clearly grows out of his poetry, from which he learned to see clearly and to verbalize what he saw, and from which he learned the subtle device of praising by naming that makes his prose so vivid. Perhaps most important, the careful reader can see his sensitive awareness of the tragedy and terror of human existence, an awareness that underlies and even gives rise to the reticence and indirection of the poetry and to the humor of the fiction. Critics who have missed this underlying sad consciousness of the human predicament in Davis's fiction, and there have been several, cannot have known his poetry.

CHAPTER 3

The Short Prose

SOON after Davis began to publish poetry in 1919, he was writing review essays for Harriet Monroe's *Poetry*. By 1927, as his work began to include narrative poems, he was also experimenting with short stories and prose sketches of the people and the landscape of the Pacific Northwest. From 1929 to 1947, almost all of Davis's published work, with the exception of his first novel, *Honey in the Horn*, took the form of short stories and sketches. This period of concentration on short prose gives that prose dual significance: both as a broad form that represents some of Davis's best artistic achievement, and also as a major transitional form in which Davis began to develop some of the primary themes he was to use in the novels that represent the apex of his writing career.

The short prose falls generally into four major groups: short stories, sketches, essays, and critical writing. Although the distinctions separating these categories may at times be arbitrary, the groups have a chronological as well as a formal principle of division. Only the critical essays were written at times ranging through Davis's entire career as a writer. The other types, which were concentrated in specific periods of his life, represent stages in his development.

Most clear cut of these groups is that of the short stories, all but one of which were published in the years 1928 through 1941. Although the works classified in the bibliography as sketches and essays frequently contain anecdotal accounts that are dramatized in the telling, only the short stories put primary interest on dramatized development of character in some unified experience that leads to a coherent effect. For example, the sketch "A Pioneer Captain" tells *about* a leading Oregon pioneer, Jesse Applegate; on the other hand, the short story "Old Man Isbell's Wife" dramatically presents the significance of a pioneer's experiences to the generation that comes during the pioneer's senile old age.

The distinction between essays and sketches is less clear, and is more successfully made on chronological grounds. The sketches were published during the brief period from 1929 through 1933, and the essays were written in the period from 1953 until Davis's death in 1960. The sketches are generally historical accounts of people, towns, or areas during pioneer or immediately postpioneer times. The only notable exception is "Three Hells," a more or less contemporary account of gambling spots in the United States and Mexico, but even here Davis uses reminiscence and reconstruction of the recent past. The essays of the 1950s, on the other hand, are contemporary accounts of a region and its people; and, though they contain reminiscence and historical background, the focus is clearly on the present rather than on the past.

The critical essays and reviews are related only to the extent that they all deal in some way with literature and its current condition as an art. These range in time over most of the span of Davis's career and provide on occasion useful insights into Davis's approach to his own work.

Whatever the ultimate critical evaluation of Davis as a writer, however, the critic who assumes that he draws only upon a folk tradition in his own childhood experience cannot have read his works carefully—and most certainly does not know of any of Davis's own critical writing. Davis knew the Classical writers, particularly the Romans, as well as the literatures of Spain, France, Italy, Germany, and Latin America. Robinson Jeffers in 1926 wrote Harriet Monroe that Davis was amazingly widely read. Davis had quoted to Jeffers a passage in Dante's *Paradiso* that Jeffers "didn't know anybody, even the translators," had read.[1] In a journal entry for December 25, 1931, Davis even laments, "I am and always have been to my severe injury, more interested in criticism than in creative writing." He says that even in his own work he too often functions better as a critic after the fact than as a creative writer at the time of composition. Perhaps Davis is overstating the case, but this comment does indicate his continuing interest in literary tradition and the principles of criticism.

I   The Critical Writing

Davis's early critical writing consisted of a few reviews for *Poetry* magazine in which he showed himself to be a careful, clear-eyed critic who was unafraid to find fault, gently, even in the poetry of

Robinson Jeffers, if he thought there was fault to be found. In his 1928 review of Jeffers's *The Women at Point Sur,* Davis formulates a basis for his own work when he objects to Jeffers's cold view of human depravity. The poet, he says, must remember that he is human and not a mindless, impersonal force like the planets. The great poem, Davis says, must be an act of love, "neither ignoring nor despising our frailties, but pitying us and them."[2]

Davis's *Status Rerum* (1926) undoubtedly attracted the greatest attention of all of his critical writing. As an assault on the age-old tendency of second-rate artists to establish mutual-admiration cliques, which review and praise each other out of all proportion to their artistic accomplishment, *Status Rerum* provides little in the way of critical theory. Aside from defining Davis clearly as a renegade from Northwest "literary society," *Status Rerum* functions more as a biographical bench mark for Davis's departure from Oregon than it does as an artistic development in itself. It is the clearest single demonstration of Davis's lifelong refusal to play social and political games to promote his career, and of his rejection of literary preciosity and affectation.

Of Davis's few later critical essays, the most significant is "The Elusive Trail to the Old West," which was published in the *New York Times Book Review* in 1954[3] and later reprinted as the preface to *Kettle of Fire.*[4] In this brief essay he establishes both a basis for the development of the literature of the American West as affected by the West's history, and a basis for the novelist's approach to his material. The West as a literary subject, he says, was a case first of rapid and then of arrested development. Settlement before the Civil War was stimulated by such factors as the dispute with England over the Oregon territory and the gold rushes in California, Nevada, and Colorado. Since what was happening in the West was of national interest, the region "got off to a better start than it was able to live up to" (13).

The Civil War stopped that interest and drew attention back to the South and East, where the war was being fought. Even after the war, literary interest focused on the South: on writers from the South who could write about what it had been like before the war, and on writers from the North who went down to write about what it was like after the war. Even Mark Twain left the West, where he had enjoyed early success, and wrote about the antebellum Mississippi of Tom Sawyer and Huck Finn. This new interest in the old South, Davis believed, came from the obvious break with the past created by the Civil War. At the heart of most American writing, Davis says, was the fact that a layer of time, of history, must be present between the writer and his material before that material becomes manageable in a literary work. The writer who tries to deal with events immediately around him has neither the perspective nor the opportunity to select the meaningful from the total flux of events and to show the patterns that have proven significant. The writer working with the vanished past, on the other hand, can judge and select more discriminately. His own memory, his own feelings about those memories, must be part of his attitude toward his material and help determine how he treats it. This view corresponds well with Davis's own best writing, which is uniformly about his native region during the years of his own childhood.

In the West, Davis says, the nineteenth century provided no clear transition such as the Civil War. Indian wars, mining and land booms, cattle drives, and the rest went right on after the war much as they had before; and Western fiction missed them all because, for the most part, "the plots twitter along on the level of sewing-circle gossip" (15). Finally, when that early West was dying, a few writers such as Theodore Roosevelt, Frederic Remington, Owen Wister, and Alfred Henry Lewis discovered some of the real material there for fiction. They were able to understand some of the significance of what the West had been at about the time when that West was slipping into the past and another West was taking its place. Other writers about the West "have been dipping out of their rain barrel for at least the last fifty years" (16).

Such "dipping" might have gone on indefinitely, but the West continued to change and the old past that was completely dead by the beginning of World War I was replaced by the new past of the first half of this century. Now the serious writer about the West must take into account not only the older West of open, empty land and pioneering adventure, but also the more recent West of crowded towns and dwindling resources. Furthermore, he must find the connection between the two and the relationship of both with the present; for they are all "a consequence of something that has happened somewhere" (17). Writers now must search through the early past and the recent past to find the links between them that earlier writers about the West seem to have missed, and to relate them both in meaningful and illuminating ways with the present.

Thus the situation of the modern serious writer about the West provides both a special problem and a microcosm of the situation of any writer of any time and place. This special problem, joined with the writer's universal problems, was the fact of which Davis was fully conscious in his writing. Although the volume of his critical writing is slight, and scattered over nearly forty years, it clearly demonstrates two major bases for his own poetry and fiction. First, he was a conscious artist who was writing from a familiarity both with folk material and with the broad literary tradition, and drawing upon both sources for his own work. Second, although he draws upon the landscape and sometimes uses the fiercest irony in his work, he considers literature to be an undertaking requiring humanity, understanding, and love—an art by which the writer helps his readers to realize most fully the depth and range of their own lives.

II   *The Short Stories*

Davis began experimenting with short stories about 1927, and he first published one under his own name in 1929.[5] With the exception of the anomalous "Kettle of Fire," written in the late 1950s[6] and published in 1959, he abandoned the writing of short stories in 1941. Between 1928 and 1941, however, Davis made a significant portion of his living from his short stories, many of which he sold to *Collier's* and to the *Saturday Evening Post*, and he began in them the development of some of the major themes he later used in his novels.

As we might expect, dependence upon the sale of short stories to the "slick" magazines led to the writing of a number of formula "potboilers." These stories show Davis to have been a skilled craftsman who was capable of writing to given editorial requirements, but many of these stories are not of significant artistic merit. Of the twenty-six short stories he published (excluding sketches and essays), ten have substantial artistic value and deserve the continued attention of scholars and critics.[7] Although the requirements of writing for the slick magazines might lead the serious writer into bad habits, against which Davis frequently cautioned himself in his journal, acceptance by these magazines did not preclude literary excellence. Even with the pages of the critically more prestigious *American Mercury* open to Davis until Mencken left its editorship, some of Davis's best short stories were published in the better-paying "slicks."

The list of slick-magazine stories that do not rise above the level of the potboiler includes "Wild Horse Siding" (1931), "Wild Headlight" (1933), "Spanish Lady" (1934), "Shotgun Junction" (1934), "The Vanishing Wolf" (1935), "A Horse for Felipa" (1935), "Railroad Beef" (1935), "Mrs. Elmina Steed" (1936), "Cowboy Boots" (1936), "World of Little Doves" (1941), and "A Sorrel Horse Don't Have White Hoofs" (1941). These generally slight stories depend on standard formula action.

Even the stories with a more serious artistic purpose and not destined for the slick magazines do not always succeed. "The Brown Stallion" (1929) has the smooth prose style so characteristic of Davis and presents a convincing picture of the countryside, but the structure of the story is not well integrated and does not lead convincingly into the conclusion. Davis has the same problem with "Cow-town Widows" (1929), in which he explores the nature of life for a widow in a little cow town in Oregon: he makes his central figure too extraordinary to be either representative or completely believable. Since he has not yet achieved full control of his flair for frontier tall tales, this story comes off as neither fable nor realistic picture. "Murder Story" (1933) is more convincing but finally never gets the reader close enough to the central figure for real involvement, and "Hell to Be Smart" (1935) has similar difficulties. We must conclude from these that, during the years in which these short stories were written, Davis was still not completely in command of his medium, at least not consistently. Pare Lorentz has suggested that Davis's short-story period was a time when he was seeking a form of expression for what he had to say. What he was trying to express, Lorentz suggests, was too large and complex to compress into the short-story form and so led inevitably to the novel.[8] Certainly such a view is consistent with the nature of the failure of some of Davis's serious short stories.

In those stories of artistic worth, three major themes recur. The most common and significant centers around human dignity, endurance, and love for other individuals and for society. Treatments of these themes may be found, for example, in "Flying Switch" (1930), "Extra Gang" (1931), "Beach Squatter" (1936), and "A Flock of Trouble" (1941). Two of Davis's best, "Open Winter" (1939) and "Homestead Orchard" (1939), are primarily initiation stories about boys who are learning their own nature and its relationship with the world around them. Finally, in "The Kettle of Fire" (1959), Davis presents an ironically Promethean theme that tries to deal, not altogether successfully, with the whole range of dignity, love, endurance, initiation, and social obligation in a symbolic, mythologized pattern. A more detailed discussion of a few of these stories will illustrate these themes.

"Old Man Isbell's Wife," the first story published under Davis's name, is a remarkably mature and polished work. In this story Davis focuses on a pair of grotesques: a doddering, senile old man who can neither button his fly nor wipe the food out of his whiskers, and a hugely fat, bewhiskered young woman. Without denying their grotesqueness or sentimentalizing their relationship, Davis gives them dignity and significance. Without softening any of the harsh outlines of boorish senility, the author says that we must honor an old man for what he has been and done, regardless of what he has become with age. By so doing, we establish a link with the past, a bond with the best of any time, and we acknowledge that courage and endurance and resourcefulness earn a man respect that time and age and failing faculties should never be able to take away. By giving respect to such qualities, we can participate to some extent in that courage, resourcefulness, and endurance and make them our own.

The irony of illustrating such a theme with absurd social outcasts comes not from cynicism but from an assertion of love that can pull even the extremes into the circle of humanity. The humor itself becomes an affirmation of this fact. If there is hostility or satire in the story, it is directed finally toward the townspeople—the smug, the satisfied, the safe. These people take neither moral nor physical risks for their lives, but they ostracize the likes of Old Man Isbell and his wife, who have to take such risks and who, in taking them, rise to a human dignity and worth that the townspeople can neither achieve nor understand.

The technique and the structure of "Old Man Isbell's Wife" are simple and straightforward. The story is told by a first-person narrator who does not himself participate in the action but whose mother plays a secondary role as a neighbor and confidant of Mrs. Isbell. The story is divided into five parts: the first describes the town and how it came to be what it was; the second describes Old Man Isbell as town dotard and bore and details the intentions of the women of the town to have him "put away"; the third presents the fat woman and tells, through conversations with the narrator's mother, of her trials as the old man's wife; the fourth presents the day of the old man's death; and the final section shows the aftermath of his death and how the fat woman has derived fulfillment from the past that rises above her ridiculous fatness and his foolish senility.

By varying his method of presentation, Davis carefully controls the dramatic action through the five sections in such a way that it builds to a dramatic climax in the death scene. The first section is pure description similar to that of his later sketches and essays. At this point, the narrator is without identity or relationship with the subject, and there are no scenes and no dialogue. Although the second section focuses more specifically on one man rather than on a whole town, the method of presentation remains the same—narrative and description without a dramatic scene. Not until the third section is the central figure, Old Man Isbell's wife, introduced. Davis then begins to build the intensity of focus by introducing dramatic scenes into the narrative, scenes of conversation between the wife and the narrator's mother. In the fourth section, the dramatic intensity reaches its height in Old Man Isbell's raving as he nears death and in his wife's participation in his memories as they flare to the surface of his delirious mind. This entire section is a single dramatic scene that ends with the woman in exhausted sleep beside the corpse of her husband; and the climax of the action of the story has been passed. The final section, the shortest, lacks action; but it is nevertheless presented dramatically as another conversation between Old Man Isbell's wife and the narrator's mother. This conversation establishes both the meaning and the significance of what has happened in the story.

A sense of the unity of the past and the present also underlies "Shiloh's Waters" (1930), but the technique of presentation is quite different. Again there is a first-person narrator, this time with a direct involvement in the narration; but Davis also uses a series of secondary narrators. He sets a scene and creates a situation in which a group of men try to explain their feelings about the wheat harvest, each by telling a story about his experiences. The resulting cycle of folk tales is so arranged that each presents an aspect of the universal human experience that the men are trying to explain to themselves. Each tale in turn circles that experience and moves in closer to its heart, just as the harvesters of the story have circled the hilltop of wheat, impatient to reach its crest. The final story in the series compares the youngest harvest hand's reaction to the harvest with his memory of his grandfather's account of moving up with reinforcements after the first day of the Battle of Shiloh. This comparison penetrates finally to the center of the experience. It explains how the emotions of the harvest hands go far beyond their knowledge of the material significance of the wheat itself or their feelings toward the old man who owns it. As in most of Davis's short stories, the final human dignity and significance come from endurance and devotion to something outside of self—to some cause, some task, some other human, or even society.

Most of Davis's best stories deal from one side or another with this question of human significance through love. In "Flying Switch," a not completely successful story about railroading, three old men find their own dignity and significance in their need for each other and their personal loyalty as they work together on a section of railroad track. The story falls short because the central figure, Stub Johnson, is not the center of the action; Johnson yields the center of the story not so much to another character as to the action itself. This eclipsing of character by action was one of the major hazards Davis continually faced in writing for magazines.

"A Flock of Trouble" (1941—renamed "The Stubborn Spearmen" when the stories were collected) shows the dignity of a man who knows his "calling" and sticks to it, even when it doesn't pay, because he does it well and it needs doing. The story also develops the images of life on the land as a battle and of the sheepherders as an army. These images' earliest statement is in "Old Man Isbell's Wife."

The problem of racism, of men who are outcasts in their own land, is added in "Extra Gang." The narrator is a young white man who works as a timekeeper under a white foreman for a gang of black railroad track laborers. At the outset, he sees the workers as "niggers," as misfits sent by a Kansas City labor broker, who do little or no work. With the usual stereotyping, the blacks are described in standard Southern racist terms of the 1930s. When one of them is seriously injured and is in danger of bleeding to death, the young narrator is put in charge of a handcar gang of the workers with orders to take the wounded man to town for a doctor. As he watches the injured man endure his pain with calm courage, the narrator's point of view subtly begins to shift. From this point the black man becomes not a "nigger" but a "wounded boy," a "wounded youth," and a "wounded man." Once in town, the narrator encounters a series of racist rebuffs in his efforts to get a doctor and shelter for the injured man. The man can have no decent shelter even though he is critically hurt; and even the doctor, when finally located, is reluctant about treating him.

As the rebuffs mount, the narrator understands more of the dignity and endurance of the injured black man and makes common cause with him: "I had been raised in that wheat-country, and I had written poems about it and some of the people in it. They hadn't shrunk any, but it seemed they had. . . . In the wounded youth alone, I had discovered more about a good way to live than they would ever know in their lives. . . . We were all broke and bedeviled, and we were, therefore, all better than the people who bedeviled us."[9] The experience causes no change in the overt relationship between the narrator and the black men of the crew, even though he openly identifies himself with them by refusing to accept shelter for the night when they can find none. No new friendships are formed, no crusades are begun; only in the understanding of the young timekeeper is there any change of which we are aware, and even the ultimate effect of that is not spelled out.

In both "A Flock of Trouble" and "Extra Gang," the point-of-view character is a boy or young man for whom the events of the story become a type of initiation into an adult awareness of certain human relationships. This theme is made most explicit in two of Davis's best short stories, "Open Winter" and "Homestead Orchard," both of which present an initiation experience for a boy on the threshold of manhood as he works with an older man. In a letter to Thayer Hobson, Davis says that "Open Winter" is the first of a series of stories using a basic pattern.[10] In this pattern, the objective is to bring the narrative finally to a single sharply drawn scene and, at the same time, "to bring the character development out on one single clear emotion." The scene is to be made memorable by the emotion; the emotion, concrete by the scene.

"Open Winter" presents a boy and an old man who are driving a herd of horses across the drought-stricken high country of eastern Oregon. The horses are not theirs, and the owner may not even pay them wages for bringing the horses through the arid high country to a safe haven on the river. In a reversal of the expected pattern, which Davis later develops more fully in *Winds of Morning*, the boy, Beech Cartwright, is the cold-eyed pragmatist, and the old man, Pop Apling, is the sentimental idealist. The boy wants to live up only to the minimum letter of his agreement with the owner of the horses. When that point is reached, he wants to abandon the horses as a hopeless undertaking. The old man, on the other hand, insists upon getting the horses to their owner, against all odds, against all practical considerations, even though the horses appear to be worthless and the owner appears not to care what happens to them. As the old man works to hold the boy to the task, he does not give idealistic or sentimental reasons. He only makes cryptic references to some value to be gained by the boy, telling him that getting the horses through will be a favor to the boy himself. Refusing to explain the nature of that favor, he merely tells the boy that he will understand when the time comes. This understanding is the initiation for which the story destines the boy; but, in the meantime, the old man also changes.

The boy's cynical, self-sufficient attitude at the outset would have made impossible the experience to which the old man so cryptically refers, but in the course of the story the boy moves steadily toward acceptance of relationships and responsibilities outside of himself. The first step in this movement is acceptance of a sense of loyalty toward the old man when the boy discovers that sheep men are looking for the horse camp to shoot the horses. Beech knows that old Apling is likely to get hurt in such an encounter; so, even though he is in the process of abandoning the old man and the horses, he goes back to warn Apling and help him move the horses before the sheep men find them.

Up to this point, Pop Apling, on the other hand, has acted on the basis of his conception of what he owes to his fellow men: he is obligated to save the horses for their owner even though their owner will probably swindle him; he is obligated to keep the horses from running loose and becoming a public nuisance in a year when pasture is desperately short; he even proposes to hold the horses on public land and ride around to nearby sheep camps to tell the herders that he and the horses are there. He assumes that, since he has as much right to pasture on the public lands as the sheep men have, the sheep men will make no objection and create no trouble. Early in the story, Beech makes sarcastic fun of Pop Apling's desire to be accommodating to his fellow man.

As the horse drive continues, the attitudes of the two move steadily closer together until the crucial day and night in which their attitudes meet and interchange. Finally, Pop Apling becomes belligerent and determined—for the sake of the lesson he still predicts Beech will learn at the end of the journey—and Beech becomes concerned for the accommodation with others. The day begins with old Apling neglecting to scout ahead so that he can tie back a line fence which they had to break to move the horses through. That "accommodation" causes them unintentionally to

drive the herd right through a calf-branding camp, which in turn
causes them to be shot at and raises the possibility of unfriendly
pursuit. When they arrive at a river crossing that night, with a cable
ferry as their best means for getting across, Apling is the one who
shoots the padlock off the private ferry, despite Beech's objection.
Beech is afraid the shot will be heard at a ranch or by pursuers from
the branding camp and bring trouble. Pop Apling shoots anyway:
" 'Let 'em come,' he said. . . . 'This is your trip . . . and I like to
ruined the whole thing stoppin' to patch an eighty-cent fence . . .
and that's the last accommodation anybody gits out of me till this is
over with' " (25).

The Christian symbolism of what follows should not be pressed
too hard, but it is more than coincidence that, when Beech hears
riders coming down the canyon behind him in the dark, dawn is ap-
proaching, and he has exactly twelve horses still waiting to cross the
river. The father figure, Pop Apling, has been working through the
darkness, taking horses across on the ferry; but at dawn, with the
ferry not yet back and with a dozen horses still to get across, the
"son" drives them into the river and follows them into the water in
a symbolic immersion that terminates just at dawn. The immersion
serves to evade the "branding" crew (which works in fire) and the
symbolic hellish fire of their guns.

At dawn of the following, climactic day, the biblical imagery is
more explicit. After a band of horse thieves has tried to steal the
herd and has been driven off, old Apling realizes that he and the
boy have gotten through, that they are close enough to the river for
horses to be worth stealing rather than being a burden. As the sun
rises, it sheds "a rose-colored radiance over him, so he looked flush-
ed and joyous and lifted up. With some of the dust knocked off him,
he could have filled in easily as a day star and son of the morning,
whiskers and all" (29 - 30). With typical irony, Davis creates here
the Satanic association for Pop Apling; but it is with Satan before
the fall, an archangelic Satan. Or perhaps it is with a Satan finally
saved: the old man and the young have brought the herd through a
winter landscape to the rebirth of spring by the river.

They have come through drought and desolation, through a
wilderness of trial and temptation, to a new life; and at that point
occurs the final realization that Apling has been promising Beech,
the experience that made the trip more important than the new-
found value of the horses or any wages he might have earned: "The
street of the town was lined with big leafless poplars that looked as

if they hadn't gone short of moisture a day of their lives; the grass under them was bright green, and there were women working around flower beds and pulling up weeds, enough of them so that a horse could have lived on them for two days" (31 - 32).

As Beech rides through town, he sees a Chinese clipping grass, and lawn sprinklers spraying water on the ground; the store windows are full of new clothes and fruit and bread and candy and hams; and, finally, the women caution their children "not to get in the man's way." He sees young people of his own age who don't know what it means to live "where there were delicacies to eat and new clothes to wear and look at." They have no sense of the comfort of being "warm and out of the wind for a change, what it could mean merely to have water enough to pour on the ground and grass enough to cut down and throw away" (32).

As the ride through town ends at the corrals by the river, where Pop Apling, appropriately for the Christian symbolism, opens the gate, Pop asks Beech if he has had enough of riding through town. He warns him it will not be the same a second time. Beech replies that it was enough; he wants nothing to be the same the second time. Beech, who has wandered through the wilderness, has won his way to an Edenic land of plenty; but he has done so only after his new sensitivity to his fellow men has made him fit for such a land and enabled him to recognize its full meaning more completely than those who had never been in the wilderness.

The Christian symbolism is much more complete and essential to the story in "Homestead Orchard." In a rudimentary outline, this Edenic story presents a return to the Garden of the second Adam, Christ, although the fable is not worked out in such flatly absolute terms. The story begins *in medias res* with a father and a son who are wanderers, outcasts, herding sheep in the rock breaks of Boulder Canyon. The father, who has alkali blindness from their time on the desert, cannot see to help with the sheep; and the son has to handle the flock alone.

The two are exiled to the wilderness because they have lost their homestead, with its homestead orchard, through the sin of the son, brought about partially by the oversight of the father and the Satanic pressures of a rancher who wanted the homestead left as open range. The Adamic fall of the son, Linus Ollivant, comes when he unintentionally shoots one of Lucas Waymark's ranch hands in an effort to protect the orchard from Waymark's cattle. What was intended as a warning shot hits the cowboy because Linus's father had kept a rifle around with sights that were knocked out of line. This fall from grace, provoked by Waymark and made possible by the elder Ollivant's carelessness, causes the Ollivants, both father and son, to be banished from the Eden of the homestead, the primeval dwelling place in the "new country."

Years of wandering follow for the father and son (no mother is ever mentioned), but they lead finally to sheepherding in a disastrously drought-stricken year that drives the flock with the blinded father and discouraged son back to the neighborhood of the homestead. At this point, the third element of the Trinity joins the father and the son in the person of Dee Radford, a herder who "ain't never worked this country before" (93) but who can see in the dark even to the extent of finding lost sheep in brush in unknown country at night.[11]

The second confrontation with the Satanic Waymark, brought about by the return to the homestead orchard, the original Garden in an unpeopled world, threatens the overthrow of Radford. The Adamic Linus's fall had originally centered on a gun, a power for good or evil that he uses unintentionally for the evil of wounding a man; and significantly, the first step in the planned overthrow of Radford is separating him from his rifle, which he had earlier hung "ceremoniously" on a fence post (102). The son's salvation at this point also centers on a gun, the one that had originally caused his fall. This time he uses it to save Radford, and he does so with the knowledge that it will not shoot and therefore cannot harm anyone. The power for either good or evil has become, in his hands, power only for good. The possibility of hellish fire has been removed.

The defeat of Satan is accompanied by the resurrection of the orchard, believed dead but bursting into bloom, even before the rain that breaks the drought. With the blooming of the battered, twisted trees, and with Radford's urging, the son resolves to return to Eden: "That much of his work had not been wasted, since it had helped to bring into life a courage and patience and doggedness in putting forth such delicate beauty against all the hostility of nature and against even the imminence of death" (111). After the fall, the loss of Eden, the years wandering in the wilderness, the son, with his greatly increased stature (he can now reach the hidden rifle where his father had put it out of his reach before), triumphs over his fall and regains his father's confidence. The rebirth of the orchard is accompanied by a reconciliation between the father and the fallen Adam, who now becomes Christ, the second Adam, with whom his father is well pleased.

"The Kettle of Fire," used as the title work in *Kettle of Fire*, Davis's second collection of short prose, was the last short story published by Davis. It is both an artistic anomaly and an interesting if unsuccessful attempt to pull together and sum up most of the major themes in Davis's short stories. Both Promethean and Oedipal, the narrative presents a boy in his relationship with a father figure and with the society in which he finds himself; and it becomes finally a story of initiation. At the same time, it is full of the harsh ironies and terrors of violent and irretrievable life. At the time of the telling, the narrator is "a rundown old relic named Sorefoot Capron," a drunk who spins the same yarn in various versions to an eleven-year-old boy in a small-town newspaper office (165).

Since Sorefoot Capron tells a story in which he is the central figure, we may question his credibility; but he admits to a shooting that is at its best a foolish mistake and is at its worst a murder from ambush. Perhaps as a hint in Sorefoot's favor, we are told that he also manages the town's water system "because he was the only resident who had been there long enough to know where the mains were laid" (165). In terms of the sagebrush country, he is the only one who knows the hidden springs of life buried in earlier times beneath the town's surface. This credibility is completed in the closing paragraphs of the story in which Sorefoot makes plain his realization that his motives were personal and that the wagon train he claims to have saved was not especially worth the effort and might finally have saved itself. The concluding paragraph, which is the author's own voice and not Sorefoot's, corroborates this conclusion and makes it impossible to regard the story as a lie. Consistent with his usual pattern, Davis uses ironic humor to gain distance and perspective for his material, but not to deceive his readers. His underlying purpose is serious.

The young Capron (a name that ironically suggests both goat and capon) runs away from home because his natural parents disdain his efforts to gain knowledge in school. This parental rejection of a desire for greater knowledge is the first step in the Promethean pattern of the story. Cash Payton, the "spiritual" father whom Capron substitutes for his natural father, carries reminders of both God and the Devil in his appearance. On the one hand, he has "a bald spot on top of his head like a tonsure"; but, on the other, he has a short red beard (166). The scar across the bridge of his nose, "from having mistimed a fuse" (166), is reminiscent of another of Davis's dualistic characters, Clark Burdon of *Honey in the Horn*, one side of whose face (in the context, clearly the Satanic side) has also been scarred by an accident with explosives used in mining. In Miltonic terms, of course, both the use of an explosive and the occupation of mining suggest Satanic qualities. The ambiguity of Payton's appearance matches the ambiguity of his death, and the "cash pay" sound of his name could suggest either reward or retribution.

The circumstances surrounding Cash Payton's death are equally ambiguous. The wickiup and the small fire suggest that theirs is neither ordinary nor innocent business; the shooting comes from mistaken identity (an Oedipal overtone); and Payton's mission there is never explained as evil or innocent. It is the mistaking of the tonsure-like bald spot for an Indian headband that leads Capron to shoot, yet it is the burning of the beard by the fire that stays in Capron's mind afterward; and, remorse or not, the Promethean act of stealing fire from the father-god and of taking it back to the lesser beings in the wagon train remains Capron's fixed purpose.

The return to the wagon train with the kettle of fire becomes a kind of Gulliver's Travels, for Capron passes through areas that are dominated each by a single kind of animal; and each kind displays a single, overriding vice or foolishness. The antelopes become nuisances from innocent curiosity; the sage-rats have a self-important conviction that only their own affairs are significant ("the proper study of ratkind was rats" [182]); the owls (scholars?) are blinded by the reality of full daylight; the jack-rabbits continue their preoccupation with procreation even though their lives are a sickened agony because of overpopulation; the geese fly and spatter Capron with their filth, much like Swift's Yahoos, out of sheer, mindless indignation; and finally the Mormon crickets consist of little more than appetites.

Capron's understanding of his own motives, the summation of the meaning of the experience to him, comes to the young man as he nears the wagon train with the kettle of fire: Prometheus brings fire from the gods to mankind not for the love of mankind but for himself. He needs to be needed, to have some meaningful role in the lives of the people even if they soon forget the importance of that role. What he brings them is not fire to dry their powder—they could have gotten that in at least two other ways while he was gone, if they had found the wit or the courage to do so. What he brings them is the courage to survive and cross the desert to Oregon. Even with the mistaken and ambiguous killing of Cash Payton, the whole effort becomes worthwhile.

Even though the people of the train neither remembered nor understood what Capron had done, Capron understood what had happened. His was the universal experience of mankind: "Such things change in substance and setting, but they go on working in the spirit, through different and less explicit symbols, as they did through the centuries before emigrations West were ever heard of, and as they will for men too young to know about them now and for others not yet born. There will always be the fire to bring home, through the same hardships and doubts and adversities of one's life that make up the triumph of having lived it" (189).

In an undated journal entry, Davis warns himself against letting a moral issue determine the plot and action of a story. It is better, he says, "to work out the plot and let the moral issues follow." This comment clearly indicates Davis's concern for the presentation of moral issues in his writing. Thus Davis concludes by acknowledging that in "The Kettle of Fire" he has written a fable. Many of his short stories are basically fables, but this one is the first in which the veneer of authenticity and realism is so openly neglected, and in which the conclusion acknowledges the fabular nature of the work. At the end of a long, productive career as a writer of short stories, the puppeteer emerges for an instant from behind the curtain and acknowledges his presence and purpose in writing about the hardships and doubts and adversities of life that comprise the triumph of having lived it.

III   *The Sketches*

The sketches of Davis deal with an individual character, a region or place, or a community and its ways. Although the distinction between Davis's short stories and his sketches is not always clear, the sketches have in general a less pervasive story line; characterization is less fully developed through action; but, on the other hand, they consistently include fictional elements. However, Davis himself does not appear to have made this distinction that we are making between sketches and short stories. When *Team Bells Woke Me*, a selection of short prose, was published in 1953, he included in the collection with ten short stories three sketches: "Back to the Land—Oregon, 1907," "A Town in Eastern Oregon," and the title piece, "Team Bells Woke Me." In his introductory note to the volume, Davis refers to the entire volume as "stories."

Indeed, according to Davis, one of these sketches marked the beginning of his career as a writer of prose. In the introductory note

to *Team Bells Woke Me,* he writes that H. L. Mencken, in accepting one of his poems for the *American Mercury* in 1928, urged him
to try prose. His response was an outline of what was to become "A
Town in Eastern Oregon." Because of Mencken's continued urging
between the submission of the outline and the completion of the
final version of the sketch, Davis says, he began writing short
stories.[12]

The other works that we here classify as sketches were all published in the five-year period 1929 - 33, and include "The Old-
Fashioned Land—Eastern Oregon" (1929), "Back to the
Land—Oregon, 1907" (1929), "A Town in Eastern Oregon" (1930),
"Water on the Wheat" (1930), "Hand-Press Journalist" (1930),
"Three Hells: A Comparative Study" (1930), "A Pioneer Captain"
(1931), "Team Bells Woke Me" (1931), "The Last Indian Outbreak: 1906" (1933), and "American Apostle" (1933). Of these ten,
only two ("Three Hells" and "The Last Indian Outbreak") deal
with topics not primarily set in the Pacific Northwest. The others all
have to do with places and people in Oregon during the years
between the time of the first settlement and World War I.

The first of these published, "The Old-Fashioned Land—Eastern
Oregon," is a sympathetic description of the sagebrush country and
the people around Antelope. Although the writing is neither stiff
nor sentimental, there is relatively little irony, and the writer's
affection for the people and even for the place is allowed to show.
This affection is not shown in the next two sketches, "Back to the
Land—Oregon, 1907" and "A Town in Eastern Oregon." "Back to
the Land—Oregon, 1907" presents an ironic and uncomplimentary
picture of early twentieth-century homesteaders who still hope for a
new start, a new promised land, an agricultural Eden. With this vision before them, they do not see the harsh realities of their situation; and their blindness leads them repeatedly to choices that make
their situation worse. Moving their wagons in the worst of the
spring mud, settling and plowing the land that has value only as
open range, stealing cattle to keep from starving while preaching
Christian pieties, the homesteaders are left neither with the dignity
of a worthy dream nor with the heroism of a great cause. Even their
dogged endurance finally has a meanness about it that keeps it from
redeeming their blind foolishness. The final complaint that they
have not yet found the country where a man stands a chance puts
the men in the same category as their ragged, dirty children who sit
in the rain-soaked wagons and cry through their noses without

opening their mouths. They are too intrinsically pitiful to have any shred of dignity.

Davis finally draws parallels between the nature of the homesteaders and that of the animals associated with them. The pack rats found in their abandoned cabins are as foolishly and pointlessly wasteful of energy, for they leave useless projects unfinished only to begin new ones that are equally useless. The cats that go wild from their homesteads become arrogant nuisances around cow camps. Only the old gray gander, surviving for years on an abandoned homestead in spite of predators and man, gains any respect from Davis and thereby surpasses the homesteaders: "If the homesteaders had possessed half his determination—" (169). Such use of animals is similar to their more openly symbolic use in "The Kettle of Fire" as illustrations of types of human folly.

In the same tone, Davis presents the townspeople of the region in "A Town in Eastern Oregon." The tone and point are the same, but the humor is lighter and more pervasive. Davis calls this sketch an astringent and irreverent commentary and recalls that it "stirred up something of a hellaballoo among the newspapers of the region" (xi). With the reputation Davis had already established as an iconoclastic critic of the Pacific Northwest, the newspapers of the region were more than usually sensitive to Davis's ironic barbs.

The town that Davis calls "Gros Ventre" in this sketch was The Dalles, the home of his adolescent years. Because both his physical description of the place and his account of its history, while tailored to fit the dramatic structure of his sketch and the humorous development of his point, apparently came too close to actuality to be either ignored or easily laughed away, the reaction was vigorous. Yet the reader whose perception is not clouded with emotion sees a smiling sympathy beneath the pointed laughter and also an acknowledgment of the heroism of people who stick to principle whatever the cost. The various groups of people the town had tamed or driven out are hardly presented sympathetically. The Indians who "shot up and butchered small emigrant trains . . . needed, perhaps, to be well thrashed" (178). The long-line freighters "were a mob of rough, ill-mannered savages" (182). The steamboat men were "too wild to control, too numerous to whip, and, by a very slim margin, too human to shoot" (184). Some of the townspeople's projects for regaining prosperity may have been foolish, but Davis sees a certain dignity in their determination to "hope and endure" (191).

Three of Davis's sketches are of individuals: "Hand-Press Journalist," "A Pioneer Captain," and "American Apostle." "Hand-Press Journalist" obstensibly presents the editor and publisher of a small-town weekly newspaper for whom the narrator has worked, but reminiscent of the "character" essays of the seventeenth and eighteenth centuries in England, this sketch presents a type rather than a specific individual.

"A Pioneer Captain" deals with Jesse Applegate, a real pioneer captain who played a leading role in the early American settlement of Oregon and in the social and political life of the region after settlement; he is the same historical figure that Davis presented in his poem "Juan Chacon" (1930). "American Apostle" also presents an historical character, Wovoka, the Indian mystic who started the ghost dances and their subsequent Indian uprisings late in the nineteenth century. Although much of the essay is fictionalized, it presents the human consequences and the significance of the whole ghost-dance episode to Wovoka and the Indians involved in it.

"Team Bells Woke Me" evokes the life of the long-line freighter in the sagebrush country of eastern Oregon around the turn of the century. The details were invented, Davis acknowledges,[13] but they present the land and the people in it with an essential truth that goes beyond a mere anecdotal narration of actual events. More than that, Davis presents aspects of universal human nature—courage, generosity, meanness, cruelty, shortsighted ambition, pride, endurance—and he does so in a context that simplifies and clarifies their nature through the directness and force of the basic requirements for survival in a land still primitive.

"Team Bells Woke Me" is, therefore, more than a picture of wagon-freighting. Davis uses a series of characters to depict specific aspects of human nature by presenting each character with emphasis on certain eccentricities, much as a moralist would in a fable. All of the characters except Frank Chambeau are purely fictional, and they have been invented "mostly to bear out some moral generality I had thought of."[14] The basic format is that of a reminiscence, the interweaving recollections of the characters of the individual freighters, the past and present nature and condition of the Indians, and the significance of the freight wagons during the wool-hauling in the spring.

Tamarack Jack Pooler becomes the basic type of the good-natured, openhanded, competent wagon freighter. His strength, courage, and skill are emphasized in his practice of breaking wild horses by working them in harness (a practice Davis's father is said by Davis to have followed, using farm machinery). His generosity and forebearance are doubly illustrated in his toleration of both the ten-year-old boy who tags along on his wagon and the ill-natured old Piute Indian beggar whose drunken wish is that his benefactor be mutilated and killed.

Uncle Ike Bewley, in his determined search for an eighth wife, at the age of seventy-four, seems the stuff of crude ribald jokes; but his reason for the search, the fear that he won't live what is left of his life to the fullest, gives him an obstinate dignity. The most striking of all the grotesques in this sketch is, however, the sour-tempered Greene Tucker, whose Indian-war wound has pulled him into a lifelong stoop and created "a lifelong grudge against creation for not doing something about it" (119). Again this character could be a comic figure only, but Davis makes Tucker more: he had, after all, sustained the wound in an act of remarkable heroism in defense of others; and, without admitting a thing beyond his grouchiness, he continues to give joy to others through his fiddling. The important statement Davis has to make in this sketch and throughout his writing is that mankind is full of quirks and foolishness, but men basically love life and their fellow man even when they are not consciously aware of such love. They may possess such love in spite of themselves, but their loving is finally what gives them value.

The team bells themselves Davis uses as the central metaphor for his conception of the nature of the times and of the country, and perhaps by extension, of any human endeavor that has value. Different freighters gave various reasons for using the bells, all more or less practical and utilitarian; but Davis understands their real significance beyond any such utilitarian reasons: "The team bells were part of freighting because they sounded pretty and gave style and ceremony to the business" (124). Wagon-freighting, like many another human endeavor that requires strength and skill and courage and effort, was more than a materialistic movement of goods for pay. It was a way to focus men's energies, a way to give meaningful dramatic structure to men's lives and to express their significance.

IV *The Essays*

From 1953 through 1961 (the last was published posthumously), Davis published a series of eleven essays in *Holiday* magazine. All but two—"The Wilds of Mexico" and "Palm Springs"—deal primarily with the landscape and with the ways of life of the Pacific Northwest. Eight of them, along with the title short story, were included in *Kettle of Fire*, published shortly before Davis's death. During most of the period in which these essays were written Davis was ill. After his leg was amputated in 1956, he was never completely free of pain nor was he able to move around with ease. Under these circumstances, we might expect that this last group of essays, all written to fit the editorial needs of one magazine, would be merely perfunctory hackwork that would display a journeyman skill but very little art.

Although we find such work in some of the early short stories, and although this final group of essays may not represent the peak of Davis's achievement as a writer, they sum up his attitudes toward the specific regional landscape. In these late essays the reader can find the feeling for the landscape and the people that forms the basis for Davis's best fiction. These essays give full play to his talent for presenting the concrete scene, the colors and sounds and feel of a place—the call of a grouse in a quiet forest; the feel of a raw, sleet-laden wind off a high lake in the fall; the shimmer of yellow aspen leaves at the edge of a clump of dark spruce trees.

More important, Davis gives us the people in this landscape—the ranchers and sheepherders and fishermen—and helps us understand the variety and depth of human nature as we watch them respond to this particular landscape. And behind it all, of course, is H. L. Davis's own response to the land and the people, his own vision of their worth and significance. With his habit of fictionalizing even those accounts that pretend most strenuously to be factual, Davis in these essays, as always, is giving us a distillation of his experience that is rearranged and even recast to make clear those underlying patterns that the flux of daily experience may conceal or confuse, but that the writer perceives and presents with an art that rises above the confusion.

The style of these essays is quieter, more direct and relaxed, than that of the earlier sketches. The humor is still much the same, but it is less insistent. The abrupt violence found in earlier works is less prominent in these essays, although it is an inevitable part of lives drawn directly from the land. The subject matter of these essays might have been presented at the outset of Davis's career as an exercise in defining the ground from which most of his fiction would be drawn. Instead, these essays are the mature work of a writer who is looking back over ground already worked and who is summarizing its geography for us after the fact. They are in no sense valedictory; for, when he died, Davis was still at work on another novel. They are simply a survey of the ground up to that moment, by a man very much alive and developing as a writer, but mellowed from the younger, sharp-penned writer of "A Town in Eastern Oregon." There is perhaps even a tone of resignation at times, although more often it is a tone of the acceptance of a flawed world in which he is nevertheless determined to see and admire the moral and emotional heights to which people are occasionally capable of rising.

V *Style and Tone*

In his short prose works, particularly his stories, Davis developed the style and tone that were to be used in his novels: vigorous, unconventional, and effective use of vernacular, without the tediousness of heavy dialect.[15] Davis's "Western" style most clearly contributes to a regional flavor, but the humorously detached tone growing out of that style clearly makes the vision of human life universal.

Western rural dialect is only hinted at in a few spellings ("git" for "get" and "yourn" for "yours," for example), but these are generally semiliterate rural pronunciations found in any part of the country. More characteristic and effective are the speech patterns of the characters, drawn from the tradition of Western humor, a tradition in which the cataclysmic is mentioned casually and the trivial is made mock heroic. This tradition, made familiar by Mark Twain, carries through all of Davis's prose fiction; but it becomes even more distinct in his novels than in his earlier short stories and sketches. In this mode, for example, the Woodside brothers of "Beach Squatter" hate paying pasture charges on their stray cattle and never do it "without a lot of impassioned oratory and the most acute suffering," but when Volney Pickett pulls a gun on them, he merely "hoisted a gun loose from a wad of haberdashery," without drama, suspense, or ceremony.

This oblique, ironic Western humor prevails through both dialogue and narrative in his stories, and also in his description of people; but, when he turns to description of the landscape, the tone and the style change. The land is presented with unfeigned seriousness and wonder. Davis's poetic technique of praising by naming is given full range in his detailed descriptions of flowers, weather, rivers, and topography. When the human element is removed, or is there only as ruins from the past, the presentation is direct, graphic, and serious; there is none of the ironic humor with which Davis came to present all things human.

CHAPTER 4

Honey in the Horn

I   *The Writing*

DAVIS'S first novel did not come easily to him. As early as 1931, he was struggling with the opening of a novel, and for a year before that he was noting ideas he might use in a novel. How close his early ideas were to what was finally published in *Honey in the Horn* is not clear, but some of these at least survived in the final version. For example, the crippled Indian boy who appeared as a major character through most of the versions outlined in Davis's journal finally appeared as an important minor figure in the published novel. At one point in his journal, he proposed as a thesis for the novel, "Community life compels formation of certain fixed stripes of character. . . . Why should a community have one drunkard and not a dozen?"[1] This idea is suggested early in the published novel, but it is not the central thesis.[2] His focus continued to be on the relationship of the individual to the community, but he found a wider scope for the treatment of that subject than just the peculiarities of town "characters."

Davis apparently regarded the fall of 1933 as the real beginning of the writing of *Honey in the Horn*, although this date relegates all the exploration of ideas and the tentative openings recorded in his journal before that date to the status of false starts. From 1930 to 1933 was a period of incubation, a time during which Davis sought his first novel's central idea.

While Davis was evolving that central idea for his novel, he was also considering models for a beginning novelist to emulate. Chaucer and Fielding are mentioned, but the names of Cervantes and Mark Twain most frequently recur in his journal.[3] Thus the picaresque nature of *Honey in the Horn* seems to have been determined by the models that Davis was following during the years in which he was formulating the novel. The connection with his models consists of more, however, than just the picaresque pattern. Davis's journals show that he was also interested in how the characters created by Twain and Cervantes "lived as much in what they've read as in what they've experienced," as much in what they believed the world to be like as in what they have actually seen it to be like. In Davis's finished novel, the reconciliation of illusion and experience becomes as important for his protagonist as for Huck Finn or Don Quixote. *Honey in the Horn*, published in 1935, thus is a picaresque story of a Western Huck Finn.

II *The Story*

Honey in the Horn is about Clay Calvert, an orphan in his late teens who is trying to find his place in the adult world. The setting is rural Oregon during the first decade of the twentieth century. Clay, who is part of the household of Uncle Preston Shively, an old man who runs a toll-bridge station and a sheep ranch in the mountains of Oregon, is one of several young people there, among them an Indian boy with crippled hands. Uncle Preston's renegade son, Wade Shively, already wanted for killing his own brother, is now wanted for killing Pap Howell, a local gambler. Clay returns from saving Uncle Preston's sheep in an early winter mountain storm to learn that Wade has been captured and is in jail in town.

The sheriff wants Uncle Preston to go to town in the storm to persuade Wade to tell where he has hidden the money Pap Howell was carrying. Uncle Preston refuses. Instead, he sends Clay, with a broken pistol that he is to smuggle to Wade. Uncle Preston's idea is to trick Wade into trying a jailbreak with a faulty pistol, assuming Wade will be killed in the attempt. Clay reluctantly does as he is asked. Believing that Wade will soon be killed, Clay takes Wade's horse and leaves the valley. He wants to be clear of the whole family. When Wade unexpectedly succeeds in escaping, Clay becomes a fugitive from the law for smuggling in the weapon and a fugitive from Wade for stealing his horse, rifle, and money.

This predicament starts Clay on a wandering series of adventures that comprise the bulk of the novel. When he meets a horse trader and his family, he is attracted by their daughter, Luce, and casts his lot with them. However, he does not tell them that he is a fugitive. In a hop-picker's camp he separates from the daughter, flees the camp when a sheriff arrives looking for another fugitive, and heads for the Oregon coast. On the way, he is again overtaken by the horse trader and Luce. He and Luce then repair an abandoned cabin and spend the winter in the coastal mountains.

By spring, they have become a part of the mountain community; and, when the other settlers decide to move inland looking for better land, Clay and Luce go along. The wagon train with which Clay and Luce are traveling is overtaken by Wade Shively, who alienates Clark Burdon, a gunman who also belongs to the group. When Clay accidentally kills a young man of the train, Burdon arranges to have Wade Shively both blamed for it and kept from making accusations against Clay. Shively is taken prisoner, escapes, is caught by a posse, and hanged. This removes one threat to Clay's freedom. As the wagon train continues its journey, Luce tries to ride Clay's mare and is thrown. As a result, she becomes ill and the wagon train leaves her and Clay behind. The illness becomes a miscarriage of Clay's child. Clay leaves her alone to find help, and when he returns, she is gone. Her father, continuing to roam the country with his horse herd, has found her and taken her with him.

A period of lonely wandering follows for Clay. He meets the Indian boy again, and then finds Luce and her father at some country horse races. After the Indian boy swindles her father in a rigged race, he is found murdered by the same gun that had killed Pap Howell. Clay then realizes that Wade Shively cannot have killed Howell. By this time, the settlers have again been starved off of the land and are again on the move. When Clay rejoins them and again finds Luce, he learns that her father is dead and that she had shot Howell and the Indian boy; but he has also learned about being alone and about belonging to a community. Finally, Clay accepts his own guilt, and Luce's. With full knowledge of both the good and the evil of which people are capable, Clay and Luce are reunited and join the community of settlers.

III   *The Critical Reception*

The initial critical reception of *Honey in the Horn* was so mixed that it ranged from high praise to brusque and even supercilious dismissal. In general, the critics' comments illustrated the problems of novels about the American West in the hands of Eastern critics, as well as the usual problems of any serious, complex novel reviewed by hurried and superficial critics. Even in the favorable notices, the reviewers missed the point of the work and praised it instead for the wrong reasons: its colorful language, its humor, and its

Western local color. In effect, even their praise labeled the novel as a minor work, as a clever entertainment, or as a regional novel about the picturesque Northwest.

Perhaps the most supercilious treatment appeared in the *Spectator*, for the reviewer discussed other novels just published with some critical acumen but dismissed *Honey in the Horn* as unread. His explanation for this neglect of the basic duty of the reviewer is only his "complete inability to read 'Western' novels." To stress his condescension, he adds that an "amateur of this kind of fiction" had assured him that *Honey* "is an unusually good example of the genre."[4]

Reviewing *Honey* for *The Nation*, Mary McCarthy objected to "the unflagging, chest-thumping virility of Mr. Davis's style"; but, as a condescending Eastern critic, she allowed that his "prose transcription of the Western drawl is occasionally amusing."[5] In a less provincial, more perceptive evaluation of the work, Malcolm Cowley felt that the plot and the characterization of the novel were weak, but he praised the "salty" characters and the descriptive prose. He later took McCarthy to task for her condescending review, calling her a literary snob.[6]

In Davis's home region, the reception was even more hostile. Another Oregon novelist might have received enthusiastic reviews in his home state, but after *Status Rerum* and "A Town in Eastern Oregon," Northwestern reviewers expected Davis to show irreverence toward their pioneer past. As a result of this regional supersensitivity, they missed the real sympathy that Davis showed toward Oregon's latter-day pioneers. Instead, they pounced upon every passage that might be taken as less than complimentary, and they stretched the question of authenticity to the point of quibbles over trivia. Newspapers published indignant editorials, Davis received abusive and threatening letters, and the major book wholesaler in the area, according to Davis, refused to stock the book at all.[7]

Davis did not consider himself a "regional" writer but a serious writer about the human condition who used regions with which he was acquainted as settings for his work. Davis considered talk of a regional novel to be "malarky." Long before the writing of *Honey*, he had observed that life in the Pacific Northwest was comparable in quantity, scale, and variety, to that in Western Europe, yet he found that no critics or reviewers considered the "Western European" novel as a genre. "Of all the traps for ruining Pacific

Coast writers the deadliest is costume and dialect—briefly, local color."[8] It must have been wryly amusing and frustrating to Davis to find that reviewers praised his first novel for just such characteristics.

On the other hand, Davis himself must bear some of the blame for this narrow reading of his work. In his prefatory note to the novel, undoubtedly with tongue in cheek, he made a statement that reviewers interpreted as his serious intention. In that note, Davis said that he had once hoped "to include in the book a representative of every calling that existed in the State of Oregon during the homesteading period—1906 - 1908." He claimed that he had given up that objective only because of lack of space. Perhaps because the novel matched their preconceptions, Davis's unwary critics took him at his word and read the novel as if he had literally meant to make the novel little more than a local colorist's catalogue of occupations.

Clifton Fadiman, who was conducting the book-review section of *The New Yorker*, attacked the novel on a number of points in a lead review in his column, and he also continued to carry a brief negative notice at the end of his column for six weeks afterward.[9] To Fadiman, it was not a novel but merely a collection of anecdotes. Reading it, he maintained, was like listening to a man who runs an information booth. His fiercest attack, however, was on social grounds. He felt that the novel had too many eccentrics, and that Davis was merely presenting degeneracy and violence to make his readers laugh. That degeneracy and violence were prime avenues to risibility suggests that Fadiman had a warped and negative view of the readers Davis might be trying to reach.

Not all the reviewers were, however, as easily misled as Fadiman. The reviewer in the *Times Literary Supplement* (London) for August 29, 1935, makes the obvious comparison between Davis's humor and that of Mark Twain, and he adds that Davis comes off well in the comparison because of "a certain subtlety and restraint even in the author's broader effects." Perhaps the fullest, most perceptive review came from Robert Penn Warren in the *Southern Review*. He felt the story was sufficient to keep the book from becoming merely picaresque. Not fooled by Davis's prefatory note, he understood clearly that the novel was more than just "a Baedeker of Oregon back-country." He, too, saw Davis as following in the humorous style of Mark Twain, but he also realized that Davis was not primarily a humorist: "humor is simply the basic way

in which he asserts his objectivity and his control of his material."[10]
Apparently without knowing Davis's poetry or the problems of
reticence and control that Davis had struggled with as a poet,
Warren accurately analyzed the deeper use that Davis was making
of humor as a way to attain greater distance and objectivity in
treating material that probed deeply into human experience. Davis
felt Warren's review was the most intelligent of the lot.[11]

H. L. Mencken was enthusiastic about *Honey*. In a letter to Davis
soon after publication of the novel, Mencken called it the best first
novel to be printed in this country, and the best novel to appear
since the publication of Sinclair Lewis's *Babbitt*.[12] He predicted a
good reception for it except from the Marxist critics, and several
comments in Davis's journals for a number of years indicate that he
felt the novel was a frequent target for attack from Marxists. Nearly
four years later Mencken's enthusiasm continued to the extent of
calling *Honey* better than John Steinbeck's *The Grapes of Wrath*.[13]

The most widely recognized support for the novel, of course,
came in the form of the Harper Novel Prize in 1935 and the Pulitzer
Prize in 1936. These awards and the resulting publicity put *Honey*
through several printings and clearly offset much of the negative
effect of unfavorable or unperceptive reviews, but they did little to
change critical opinions. These awards made the novel impossible
either to ignore or to forget, and they kept it alive long enough to
permit more thoughtful critical evaluation. Even so, the quantity of
critical attention has been slight. Like the reviews at the time of
publication, they are a mixed lot of good and bad.

The negative critics still dismiss the novel as local color or as
picaresque foolery.[14] The favorable treatments emphasize Davis's
use of folklore, dialect, and descriptions of the landscape. These
critics see clear connections with the American literary tradition
through both Twain and Hawthorne as well as with such contemporary Western writers as Walter Van Tilburg Clark and A. B.
Guthrie, Jr.[15] They consider Davis a significant American writer
with a place in our literary tradition, a writer who draws upon the
folk resources and the landscape in which his work is set, as did
Hawthorne and Twain and James and any other writer of serious
fiction. Yet, like any other serious writer, Davis's work speaks to the
common human experience of all times and places. It seems likely
that the number of critical works that treat *Honey* in this light will
continue to grow.

The novel now seems to have won a place in American literature as a minor classic.[16] Looking back from 1955, Davis noted with amusement that, despite the furor raised at first in the Pacific Northwest over the novel, "all the hollerers had disappeared" by the time some of the same region's reviewers came to his later novels. The newer generation of reviewers "accepted Honey in the Horn [sic] as gospel, as revelation. They invoked it reverently . . . ." Davis found this attitude embarrassing because he was aware that the novel did indeed have "inaccuracies and cheap spots." In Davis's eyes, it deserved neither the early fury nor the later unquestioning reverence.[17] In any case, the book's place in our literary tradition was by then secure.

IV *Clay Calvert and Huck Finn*

The obvious comparison of *Honey in the Horn* with the work of Mark Twain carries far beyond style and the tradition of frontier humor. The basic plot structure and subject matter suggest comparisons in some detail with *Huckleberry Finn*. In each novel, an adolescent boy journeys through a series of adventures, in a more or less picaresque context, gaining insights into the culture of a region and into the nature of mankind. *Huckleberry Finn* is clearly superior in a number of ways—in the fuller realization of the central character and in the unifying device of the river, whose flow presses the action onward and gives an irresistible movement and direction to events. But *Honey in the Horn* succeeds where *Huckleberry Finn* finally fails. Both narratives begin with a boy who is fleeing the restrictions of society. Davis's novel reaches an acceptable resolution to the central problem of the boy's relationship with society, his attitude toward and acceptance of mankind.

Huck at the end of his journey down the river, in spite of all he has seen and, presumably, learned, can only continue to flee from society by "lighting out for the territory." He ends without resolving the problem with which he began. He fears that Aunt Sally will continue to try to "sivilize" him. For an adult, to be civilized is to be made a part of a civil community; although Huck sees the process in a child's terms—having to wash and go to school and mind his manners—he is nevertheless resisting the community's effort to make him a part of it. Like Peter Pan, he wants to stay free of the obligations of adult society.

Clay Calvert, on the other hand, learns and changes; he comes to terms with society; and he is at last able to assume a place in it. He

begins his journey in flight from society and its injustice, but he
finally finds a basis for returning to it and functioning meaningfully
within it.[18] Thus Huck's flight first into make-believe, and then into
unsettled wilderness, is not necessary for Clay. He has resolved his
problem. Unlike Huck and Peter Pan, he can grow up.

V *The Story as Christian Parable*

What may at first appear to be a loosely related set of rambling
adventures evolves in *Honey in the Horn* into something very like a
morality play about man and society, about the basic problems of
good and evil, and about natural depravity and brotherly love. It is
a story about the problems of human communication, human
relationships, and the understanding and acceptance of human
nature, an initiation story in which the adventures form a series of
cumulative steps in the developing maturity and understanding of
Clay Calvert. Davis uses a series of images, relationships, myths,
and archetypal patterns to make clear the universality of his major
themes. The reader must beware of finding in these patterns a
direct, one-to-one allegorical meaning for the story, but ignoring
these patterns leads us into the error of reading only for "local
color." With these limits in mind, our examination of some of these
major patterns and their roots in our culture should develop our
deeper appreciation of Davis's art.

Clay Calvert is exactly that, the common clay of humanity, an
Adamic figure with no past, no parentage, no established place in
any human society. His father is unknown, his mother is an
itinerant outcast who bears him in a fence corner, finds shelter for a
few years with Uncle Preston Shively's outcast sons, dies, and leaves
Clay to the wild existence of the Shively boys. From such inchoate
outer darkness, Clay is adopted into the imperfect Eden of Uncle
Preston's toll station when, like Cain and Abel, one of the Shively
boys kills the other. The surviving brother becomes a fugitive outcast, for he is driven from Uncle Preston's land under threat of being shot if he returns; and he is driven from society by the law. The
mark of Cain is very real upon him.

The ironic Eden of the toll station is dominated by old, overgrown and underrooted apple trees which, like the original apple
tree in the Garden, threaten to destroy the entire establishment
every time there is a storm. The station is inhabited by a variety of
rootless orphans besides Clay Calvert: an Indian boy who, re-

nounced by his own people, refuses to accept any other; a housekeeping girl whose stomach rumbles any time her emotions are aroused; and assorted other youngsters. This group is presided over by the ironic father-figure of Uncle Preston, who is so preoccupied with recording a largely irrelevant past that he has no time to deal with the present or to provide for the future. His preoccupation with "the old days" at the dawn of white settlement in that country and his resulting willingness to let the apple trees smash the toll station suggest an ironic image of the God of the Old Testament.

In the midst of a storm that threatens to bring the apple trees down on the house, wash out the toll bridge, and destroy his flock of sheep, Uncle Preston tries to ignore the disaster threatening his kingdom. He continues work on the history he is writing of the early statutes of Oregon. When he receives word that his surviving son has been captured and stands accused not only of killing his brother but also of murdering and robbing Pappy Howell, he finally gives some attention to the present. He does so, however, only inadequately through an intermediary "son" and on what turns out to have been misleading evidence. Howell was found shot, lying in the road, with the tracks of Wade Shively's horse all around the body. The cloven mark of a broken shoe, suggesting the cloven hoof of Satan, is what identifies the horse.

As an ironic God-figure, Uncle Preston denies responsibility for the crimes of his earliest son, the Satan-figure Wade Shively. While he is trying to do so, Uncle Preston is told the story of an early settler who shot his own son to keep him from revealing to the raiding Indians the hiding place of the rest of the family. In a belated attempt to relate his beloved history to current problems, Uncle Preston accepts this story as an answer to what he should do about his son Wade. His plan to trick Wade into attempting a jailbreak with a gun that will not fire, expecting that Wade will be killed in the attempt, and his decision to make Clay, his latter-day "son," the agent of the plan, suggests the concept of the "fortunate fall." In both instances a "father" uses his children (Wade-Satan, and Clay-Adam) against each other, lays a trap deliberately tempting the transgressor to sin again (the vulnerability of Eden was necessary for the ultimate triumph of Christ), but involves his agent (Clay-Adam) in sin along with his enemy.

The failure of Uncle Preston's plan makes Clay a fugitive, but it leads him to Luce, a woman who is indeed Light—an Eve who will

bring an understanding of good and evil to Clay. Luce and a place
in the community of mankind can only be Clay's, however, after a
series of experiences, confusions, and revelations that finally force
him not only to realize man's evil nature, but also to accept it as un-
avoidable, and to accept mankind as brothers, evil notwithstanding.

Again the ironically weak father-figure is at the center of difficulty, for Clay tries to possess Luce without telling her about his own
past and what he is running from. Luce has also concealed from him
the guilt in her past from which she is fleeing, and that her guilt was
also initiated through the weakness and foolishness of a cheating,
swindling, horse-racer father. When Luce loses their child through
miscarriage, the tensions created on both sides by this hiding of past
guilt lead to an emotional "miscarriage" of their love, also, and
Clay loses Luce again to her dissolute father. In the meantime,
however, Clay's efforts to conceal his past lead him to kill one man
accidentally and to cause Wade Shively to be hanged for that and
for the accidental death of another man. Later Clay learns that the
other murder of which Wade stood accused, the shooting of Pappy
Howell, was committed by Luce. Thus in this ironic version of the
Christian story, the Satanic Wade Shively, the quarrelsome brag-
gart, is transmuted into a Christ-figure: he is hanged to atone for
the sins of mankind, of Clay and Luce, of the Adam and Eve of this
frontier world. This transformation of the outcast, Satanic Cain into
Christ the redeemer is the final realization to which Clay must come
before he fully understands human nature and the human predicament.

To make the transformation unmistakable, Davis injects a series
of circumstances with Christian associations into the death scene.
Like Christ, Wade Shively at first tries to escape his execution:
Christ, by prayer; Shively, by flight. Both are captured at night, and
both become reconciled to their deaths. Goaded by the capricious
Clark Burdon, who has now assumed the role of Satan, Shively's executioners truly know not what they do; for they believe Shively has
shot Foscoe Leonard and the Lund boy. Clay knows better, but he
still believes Shively shot Pappy Howell and knows he killed his
own brother, so he does not intervene. Furthermore, Wade
Shively's death is a belated fulfillment of the will of his "father,"
the original settler, Uncle Preston.

The physical circumstances of the hanging make the Christian
analogy more explicit. The arrival of daylight "almost as he
dropped," with the clouds overhead turning pink and the colors of

objects becoming visible, is reminiscent of the death scene in Herman Melville's *Billy Budd*, for the scene has the same associations. Wade dies without showing pain or fear but with "half-amazed triumph," and his body is wrapped in a blanket and buried "in stony ground outside the hay-field fence." Finally, driving the point home inescapably, the Basque sheepherder in whose camp Wade was captured brings out a goatskin of red wine; and he squirts some wine into the mouth of each of the lynchers, as "every man knelt on the ground" (293). This final gesture of kneeling to receive the red wine from the shepherd makes again the point of the irony of human nature by creating an ambiguous association between the nature of disciples and of executioners. These men kneeling and receiving the wine were, in effect, both exacting the atonement and benefiting from it.

To complete the parallel, Davis makes the Satanic nature of ex-gunman Clark Burdon the underlying force that drives the lynchers on to the execution. Burdon, as capricious "evil according to nature," is indeed the burden carried by every clerk, every man of the church. Burdon is deformed, and his scarred face suggests the split countenance of the Satanic stranger in Hawthorne's "My Kinsman, Major Molineux." One side of his face is normal, even handsome; but the other is only a huge, featureless scar left from the explosion of a dynamite cap he was crimping to use in a mining blast.

It is Burdon who arranges matters so that Wade Shively is hanged for the death of the man Clay has shot accidentally and for that of the man Luce has shot deliberately. As a bringer of death, as a tempter, as a man marked by hellish fire in subterranean labors, Burdon's Satanic nature is unmistakable. Yet his dual nature as carouser and executioner, as handsome man and hideous scar, and as concerned friend and callous, vengeful gunman suggests a Miltonic fallen archangel. The coherence of this ironic Christian fable gives the novel a far tighter structure than the traditionally picaresque tale might be expected to have.

As in the Christian story, reconciliation is the outcome of this parable. In this case, however, the reconciliation is between Clay Calvert, the isolated fugitive from society, and the society that is represented by a group of homesteaders. The reconciliation comes not only after Clay has learned the nature of evil in mankind, but also after he has found that same evil in himself and Luce. When he can accept the perplexing mixture of love and hate, of strength and weakness, and of cowardice and courage that is human nature, he can be reconciled with Luce and rejoin the wagon train.

VI   *Man and Animal*

Within this primary structure, Davis uses other patterns to develop his theme. For example, horses play a significant role throughout the story. Clay begins his flight from society on Wade Shively's mare. The mare, with her telltale broken shoe and cloven track, is a finer horse than a boy like Clay would be likely to own. She gives Clay freedom of movement, but she also brings trouble that forces him to continue to move. People continually question whether such a fine horse could belong to such a boy.

When Luce, a superb horsewoman, tries to ride the mare, however, she is thrown and has a miscarriage. The horse thus becomes the means of showing that Clay and Luce are not yet truly together because of their concealing their own crimes and fears from each other. The mare, a part of the redemption left Clay by Wade Shively's atonement, cannot yet accept Luce. At the end of the novel, when all fears and guilts have been revealed and accepted, the ownership of the mare is no longer questioned. She is in harness and is pulling a wagon, a sign that Clay has at last joined his option for freedom—the mare—to the needs of the community. No longer a means of flight, she is a means of helping.

Luce, on the other hand, is associated throughout the novel with her father's stallion, the horse through which her father has caused all the trouble that has led to Luce's fears and guilt. This stallion, which bears false harness galls as false claims of service to the real needs of society, is used by the trader to win mismatched horse races; and the trader's losing two bets leads to Luce's killing two men. The horse is an instrument of deception and trouble. Consistent with this pattern, Luce's attempt to lend the stallion to the community of settlers leads only to the stallion's death. Alive, it represents what stands between Luce and human community. It is the means by which she and her father preyed upon society. She must lose the stallion before she can become a full member of the community of settlers.

Associated with the horses are the figures of the horse trader and of Wade Shively. These in turn are not traditionally villainous figures. Rather, they are men separate from society who live out their own natures as they must and who finally meet their consequent lonely ends with more dignity than might be expected. The pattern is established very early, in yet another paralleling of human fortunes with animal nature, when Clay watches a coyote drive a ewe from the flock of sheep he is tending (20 - 22). After he has shot the coyote, Clay is reminded of Wade Shively, in an adumbration of Clay's role in Wade's death. This parallel between coyote behavior and characters in the novel continues, later including the horse trader and the Indian boy, too. All are outcasts, predators. When Shively escapes from the wagon train, his behavior is again compared to that of a captive coyote (281).

All die with surprising ease: Shively and the coyote die at dawn at Clay's hand; the horse trader dies because, when Luce has finally refused him help, he has become completely isolated. Pappy Howell and the Indian boy, the two "predators" killed by Luce, also die at dawn without ceremony or warning since death is neither special nor horrible; it is a natural event that comes quickly and easily. The association of Wade Shively with the ways of the coyote becomes a complete circle when Clay's strategy against the mowing competition of the Indian boy is a parallel with the strategy of the coyote killing the ewe (345 - 46). Clay's use of the coyote's tactics shows that he, too, is capable of behaving like a predator when faced with isolation. Like Adam, he carries some Satanic flaw.

Finally, the shepherd and the predator and the sheep act out their respective roles as they are given them; and none carries any special burden of guilt or obligation. The predicament of mortality becomes something to be accepted without bitterness or struggle by killer and victim alike.

VII *Initiation*

All of these elements—the Christian fable, the pattern of symbolism related to horses, the interweaving of human and wild animal behavior and motivation, the landscape and life and folklore of Oregon—contribute to the development of a basic initiation story. An alienated boy becomes a man in society; he is at peace with himself, with society, and with the human predicament; but he has full knowledge and acceptance of the evil as well as the good of which mankind is capable.

At the beginning, all of the characters in the home valley are isolated; they are trying to communicate but are unable to do so. Clay saves Uncle Preston's sheep against all odds and after two experienced sheepherders have given them up, but his achievement is ignored in the selfish preoccupation of the others with their own interests and problems of the moment. The half-breed boy's extraordinary skill driving horses on the trip into town is ignored because halfbreeds have no status in that community. The isolated settlers in the back country are so anxious to explain themselves and their experiences to others that they forget how to listen (105 - 107). Each mode of isolation feeds upon itself, insulating its victims progressively further from communication.

At first Clay seeks the same kind of isolated independence, but he cannot keep it. He wants to be free of Wade, Uncle Preston, the housekeeper, even the Indian boy who helps him; but he meets Luce and surrenders that independence when he joins the horsetrader's family to be with her. But, since he has lessons to learn, the encounter with One-Armed Savage begins his education: "The lesson in that was that bravery in the wrong place was nothing but a blamed nuisance . . ." (137). At the hop camp, he learns his second lesson, "something about what love could amount to" (153), and so his education progresses. At times he tries to ignore what he has learned and to return to isolation, but he cannot do so.

From the horsetrader's family, Clay moves to the larger group, the coast settlers who are looking for new land and a new start. When they start inland, he feels a part of something important that is more than himself: "The line of fires down the valley, the strange wagons pulling in and being directed to their places . . . , the knowledge that this was . . . an entire people . . . gathering to tackle a new country . . . gave him a feeling of dignity and strength that, though miles beyond his own reach, was his because he belonged to these people" (225 - 26).

He is learning, but there is more wandering, more trouble, and more education before the lesson is complete. He must be honest with himself and with Luce, and he must finally learn the whole truth about her and about the nature of mankind before he can genuinely join a true community. When he has accepted the fact that Luce has deliberately killed two men who probably deserved it and that he mistakenly has caused the death of two men who probably did not, when all the errors and guilts and evils have been acknowledged and accepted while still accepting the obligation of one human being to another, then Clay and Luce can join the community of settlers and become a part of the family of man. In this family, too, Clay can recognize the gamblers and sheepherders, the harvest hands and rivermen, the whores, the wheat farmers, and the drifters and laborers as brothers and sisters who spring from the same clay as himself, show the same weaknesses, and are limited by the same mortality.

VIII   *The Center in Everyman*

Perhaps the most telling criticism of the novel is that the central character is never fully realized. More than two decades after its publication, Davis acknowledged the justice of this criticism,[19] but he says the central character is incompletely developed only if Clay Calvert is the central character. Actually, he says, the main character, the consciousness with which we are finally concerned, is not Clay but the narrator, who "is felt as a part of the book, and the emotion back of the narrator is felt as a part of it." If the reader accepts the narrator and observes Clay's pilgrimage from alienation to community through the narrator's eyes, to that extent the narrator and the reader join and the central consciousness of the novel becomes the reader. In another sense, the center of the book is the problem that Clay Calvert faces, the problem of acceptance of the evil inherent in human nature.

The solution of the problem is the resolution of the conflict in the novel. In this sense Clay Calvert becomes Everyman of the morality play, or Christian of Bunyan's *Pilgrim's Progress;* and Clay therefore does not need a fully, vividly developed character. Clay and the narrator and the reader are all the same in the problem of alienation versus community. With only the outline of a character, an outline that leaves room for the inclusion of any of us, there is a continuing flow among Clay and the true narrator and the reader—a flow that allows reader identification with the problem itself. In fact, we arrive back at the novel as morality play in which we can all visualize ourselves as acting parts. In this sense, the real center of the novel becomes the universal human experience as it might have been worked out in Oregon at the turn of the century through the eyes of H. L. Davis.

CHAPTER 5

Other Times, Other Places:
Harp of a Thousand Strings

AFTER winning a Pulitzer Prize and causing a considerable stir among literary critics, Davis might have been expected to capitalize on the attention he had attracted with his first novel by hurrying another into print as quickly as possible. Instead, a hiatus of twelve years occurred before *Harp of a Thousand Strings* appeared. By that time a good deal of the public momentum for the development of his career as a novelist was lost. In fact, there was speculation that Davis was merely a "one novel" writer who had put all he had to say into *Honey in the Horn*. Critics wondered if he lacked the depth and productivity to progress beyond it, but the delay in the publication of his second novel was the result, rather, of the already described dispute between Davis and his publisher, Harpers'.

I The Critical Reception

In the twelve-year gap between the publication of *Honey* in 1935 and the publication of *Harp*, in 1947, the stir created by *Honey* had been generally forgotten. Hasty initial reactions had presumably yielded to maturer reflection about the novel; critics had had more opportunity to see beyond such superficial features as eccentric minor characters and colorful speech to the more central themes of the work. Then, too, much had changed in the critical climate of the country. The nation had emerged from a depression and had gone through the biggest war in the history of mankind. In a postwar period of peace and prosperity, ideological and social questions were no longer so clearly significant in the standards of most critics. Grimly proletarian novels were no longer the only kind given a friendly reception by a major segment of the literary community. New novels were much more likely to be judged, even if superficially, for their literary merit rather than for their ideological orientation.

In this context, *Harp* was received with mild approval as an interesting historical novel by an established writer.[1] Yet Davis was no more interested in writing "historical" fiction in the sense of using historical factors to gain interest than he had earlier been in writing "regional" local-color fiction that depended on setting, costume, and dialect. Davis, who had very firm convictions on this subject, wrote in his journal for August 19, 1955, some years after the publication of *Harp*, that, "Lapsing into historical fiction is always a sign of mental decline in a novelist." There is no evidence that he regarded the writing of *Harp* as a sign of his mental decline.

Fortunately, some reviewers saw beyond the historical surface to the underlying serious intent of the work. In fact, more reviews of this type appeared for *Harp*, than for *Honey*. Perhaps because Davis made his underlying patterns more obvious in this novel, more reviewers understood that he was presenting certain universals of human experience. There is less color, liveliness, and humor in this novel than in *Honey*, and in *Honey* these otherwise commendable qualities seem to have distracted readers from perceiving the basic patterns of meaning.[2]

II *The Story*

Harp of a Thousand Strings presents two stories, each of which is derived in turn from a number of others. The first of these two is the story of three Americans—Melancthon Crawford, Commodore Robinette, and Indian Jory (Apeyahola)—in a series of adventures that begin in Tripoli and end in their old age on the Oklahoma prairie. The second story centers on a Frenchman, Jean-Lambert Tallien, during and after the French Revolution. These two stories, in turn, flow together for a time into the story of Thérèse de Fontenay, a French noblewoman and Tallien's former wife. The novel comes to a provisional conclusion about the significance of all of these stories, but it is only provisional because every human story goes on forever, somewhere, in some form.

The novel opens in a small town on the prairie at the edge of the Osage country around the middle of the nineteenth century. Old Melancthon Crawford, one of the pioneer founders of the town, has been declared mentally incompetent at the request of his greedy relatives in the East. They fear that he will give away his money to a religious group rather than leave it to them. In spite of all the flight, the hiding, and the resistance of which the old man is capable, he is caught, forced onto a stagecoach, and carried away. That evening the other two founders of the town, Commodore Robinette and Indian Jory, walk to the site of their original trading post and reflect on what their lives have amounted to, if those lives can lead to such a pitiful event. Their conversation provides the dramatic framework for the rest of the novel.

The three men, each with a varied history of his own, first meet on the beach in Tripoli during the American bombardment of that port in 1805. They have all been prisoners in Tripoli and have been forced to serve the guns that return the fire of the bombarding American fleet. When the naval guns hit the shore batteries, the three Americans escape in the smoke and confusion. At that point, they first meet on the beach. Robinette has been wounded; the three have no plan for reaching the American fleet; and so they take refuge in a warehouse, where their planning—and quarreling—is interrupted by the arrival of Tallien, who is the French consul to Tripoli.

As the Americans await darkness for their escape, they reveal that each man has been motivated by one of three basic passions: love, ambition, vengeance. The Indian, Apeyahola, who was kidnapped into naval service, wants only to return to his wife. Robinette is ambitious for promotion and glory as a military officer, although women often lead him away from strict attention to that goal. Crawford, in turn, wants revenge on his hometown by returning to it rich and powerful. The French consul, Tallien, observes that he has served all three of those passions. To pass the time and to keep the Americans from quarreling among themselves, he begins to tell his story of what these passions have cost him.

The story of Jean-Lambert Tallien is the central one of the three major sections of the novel. Tallien was an actual historical figure who played a significant role in the French Revolution, and Davis keeps his account faithful in its major points to the historical facts. As Tallien is beginning his account, a French merchant and a veiled woman, two of the people the consul had come there to meet, arrive. Since the men still must wait, Tallien continues his story, about his rise to power, his part in the overthrow of Robespierre, and his own conduct of the government until he loses power. He attributes all of his actions during that time to three passions: personal ambition, a desire for vengeance against his native village, and his love for Countess Thérèse de Fontenay. Fulfillment of his ambition led only to greater cares and frustrations—not to greater power over his own fate. Indeed, he finds that his high office makes him more a puppet of events than a determiner of them.

His desire for vengeance became hollow and pointless because people change. The village upon which he might have taken his revenge was changed from the one that had done him the wrong. Although the same people were there, their circumstances and their attitudes were different; and he could find neither reason nor satisfaction in exacting revenge upon them. He makes Thérèse de Fontenay his wife, but the death and the suffering he has had to cause to win her and to hold her finally begin to obsess him. As this happens, he begins to lose power; and he loses her because he has not won love in return. Tallien's conclusion is that love, vengeance, and ambition are empty goals.

After Tallien finishes his story, the Americans learn that the veiled woman, who has quietly listened to Tallien's recital, is Thérèse de Fontenay. She expresses a hope that somehow her life will yet be worth the suffering it has cost, and she gives the three Americans a pair of pistols and a dagger. All three weapons are marked with her crest, an open hand holding a flower. The Americans then leave the warehouse, successfully escape Tripoli, and eventually make their way back to America.

Years later, when Robinette and Apeyahola meet again, Robinette's ambition has led only to the slaughter of disarmed Spanish troops by Texas rebels; and Apeyahola's love for his wife has ended in his killing her for being unfaithful. Both fugitives—Robinette from the Spanish government and Apeyahola from the American—make their way westward from the Mississippi River without weapons, supplies, or money. Ready to give up, they find a trail marker in the form of the Fontenay crest. Hoping to find the countess, led on by their memory of her resolve to make her life count for something, they follow the markers westward. What they find instead is Crawford, the third American from Tripoli, who, barricaded in his prairie trading post, is gravely ill. Since Crawford's dream of vengeance has also come to nothing, all three have found their goals unrewarding. All three are outcasts on the fringes of civilization, and they have no strong motivation beyond mere survival.

The rest of the plot follows easily. Robinette and Apeyahola nurse Crawford to health. The three run the trading post together and take up land claims around it. After years of such a life, a town finally grows there, and the three are regarded as its founders. This point of their story brings us to the situation with which the novel opens, Crawford's removal. What remains is the speculation of Robinette and Indian Jory about what their history finally means.

Davis finds the answer in the fact that the men have named the town after Thérèse de Fontenay. In spite of all that life had cost her, in spite of shame and bitterness and suffering, she had never feared life nor lost faith in its potential value. Her motivation had never centered on an overriding passion; she had simply accepted life as it came. Only when the three Americans had abandoned their overriding passion and had begun to choose life on its own terms had their lives produced positive values.

III   *The Basic Patterns*

Underlying the primary story line, as is usual with Davis's work, we find a complex set of allusions, associations, and symbolic patterns by which Davis relates this specific story, this particular account of human experience, to the universal human condition. By use of these devices, he speaks directly to the reader's experience in the reader's own time, place, and circumstances. By properly understanding Tallien, Thérèse de Fontenay, Commodore Robinette, Apeyahola, and Melancthon Crawford, we can perhaps better understand ourselves.

At least superficially, *Harp* is a traditional historical novel, but it is more significantly a novel about history. The image of a harp of a thousand strings occurs in a hymn by Isaac Watts published in 1707 (*Hymns*, Book II, No. 19):

> Our life contains a thousand strings
>   And dies if one be gone.
> Strange! that a harp of a thousand strings
>   Should keep in tune so long.

This verse suggests the rich tapestry of threads of which every life is woven. These threads of events, influences, and relationships come from many sources and weave many patterns. When one life is finished, its threads continue on endlessly into other lives, tying together the whole story of mankind. This continuation is exemplified throughout the novel, giving the original source of the title a particular relevance to the work.

However, Davis says he took the title not directly from Watts, but from a parody of a Southern revival sermon that had made mistaken use of Watts's imagery.[3] That sermon was first printed in *The Spirit of the Times* in 1855 and was attributed to Henry Taliaferro Lewis.[4] A version of that folk sermon provides not only the title but also an epigraph for the novel. In the sermon, the Harp is "the sperrits of just men made perfict"; the novel shows that perfection may finally happen in the sweep of history, regardless of immediate failures and losses. History becomes the harp of a thousand strings, and each string may be the story of a "just man" caught in a flow of events. His role in the story of mankind may seem in his lifetime to be a failure, but it may finally reach farther and count for more than he can realize.

The theme had evolved for Davis at least as early as 1928. In that year, in a review of Robinson Jeffers's *The Women at Point Sur*, he wrote that "Stories have actually neither beginning nor end. Every story is like a river; it began flowing with the beginning of the world, and it will not cease till the world comes to an end. I don't doubt in the least that the story of Oedipus is still going on, somewhere, at this very moment."[5] Time becomes, therefore, another dimension through which humanity is joined in a common story that is affected by the actions of all. Davis explicitly presents this concept in the text of *Harp*: "Stories change, and shift ground and directions and actors . . . but they can no more end than a river can change its identity by shifts of current . . ." (267).

History then is not determined by great men, Davis says. It is rather the story of great men being run over by humanity while trying to steer them. He formulated this principle in his journal as early as 1935. In *Harp*, caught in the political requirements of a struggle for power, Tallien encounters the same force: "It was not a question of energy that could be directed where he pleased. It was a question . . . of keeping pace with it to keep it from running over and destroying him" (196). Old Crawford's removal from the Western town that he helped to found, and had later saved from an Indian raid, suggests that history has run over and left behind not only Crawford but also Robinette and Apeyahola. Yet their deeds, like Tallien's, had helped shape its course and would continue to affect it.

Harp is Davis's most elaborately structured work, and the one in which the structural design is most obtrusive. This structure, based on a series of triads, begins with the three Americans. Each

American represents one of three basic emotions, and these same emotions are encompassed in the story told by Tallien. The novel is also divided into three sections, but this division is primarily a dramatic device that separates Tallien's story. These triads suggest Dante's divisions of Hell, ones based on Aristotle's three kinds of evil nature in humanity.[6] Aristotle speaks in *Ethics* of vice, imperfect self-control, and brutishness (*Ethics*, VII), and Dante transmuted these in his *Divine Comedy* to incontinence, malice, and brutishness (*Inferno*, XI). The love, vengeance, and ambition of Tallien and of the three Americans may not be entirely parallel, but the similarities are clear. Tallien's love for Thérèse de Fontenay is clearly a selfish love that equates well with the lust implied in Aristotle's category of vice and Dante's category of incontinence. Physical, selfish love leads Tallien to kill others to keep possession of a woman; and the same emotion causes Apeyahola to kill his own wife because she will not remain exclusively his. Vengeance equates well with malice and with imperfect self-control, because vengeance here grows out of malice and has no purpose beyond itself. Brutishness and ambition are less clearly parallel, but the merciless consigning to death of those standing in the way of Tallien's ambition and the slaughter of the Spanish troops captured by Robinette provide similarities.

Since Davis knew the *Divine Comedy* well, the parallels are undoubtedly more than mere coincidence. The continuation of the three basic emotions from Aristotle to Dante to the French Revolution to the American frontier, thereby spanning the movement westward of Western culture over two thousand years, underlies Davis's thesis that human stories never end, that there is a basic unity in the experience of all humanity.

This elaborate structuring of the plot, however, leads to excessive dependence on coincidence. Tallien's story depends on such coincidences as the chance selection of the Jacobin Club as his fictitious destination to escape Suleau's company and the presence of the Théroigne woman in front of it just at that moment. His political coup is set off by his chance encounter with Thérèse de Fontenay in a cart headed for a Paris prison. The drama of the telling of the story, as well as the point of the novel, is intensified by the chance meeting of Tallien, the Théroigne brother and sister (she insane), Thérèse de Fontenay, and the three Americans under the most extraordinary circumstances in a warehouse in Tripoli during the American bombardment. Finally, the three Americans are reunited years afterward by an equally extreme set of coincidences.

With such heavy reliance upon coincidence, *Harp* does not hold up as Realism or as what Davis at the outset presents it to be: only slightly fictionalized history. As a dramatized fable of how individual lives are carried along in the flow of human history, and the possible choices and ultimate meanings open to those lives, it works more effectively; for coincidence is more acceptable in a fable. And what this fable presents in dramatic form is the fact that individual humans are not just acting out their own private histories: they are an integral part of what is happening on the larger stage of the world. The narrative shows us that we are all a part of the larger drama of humanity, a drama that is universal not only spatially but temporally. The tide of the story of humanity rolls on inexorably, and all stories are unavoidably interlocked. In spite of personal motivations, individuals are finally captives of that tide and may have to pay a higher price for their own desires than they appear to be worth.

In Tallien's story and in the lives of the three Americans, individual purposes seem to have cost too much and to have returned too little, but the novel's point finally comes down not to Tallien or to the three Americans but to Thérèse de Fontenay and the immortality of any human story. Her range of choice was more restricted than Tallien's, but she, too, had some opportunity to gamble everything for the sake of love, ambition, and vengeance. She had an opportunity, also, to choose atonement, as did her fiancé, the young nobleman de Bercy. Yet, each time she was faced with such choices, she chose life, survival, above the others.

At the end of Tallien's recital of what her survival had cost him and others, she can still reaffirm the hope that her life, somehow and somewhere in the flow of human history, would finally be worth the price. When she gives the knife and brace of dueling pistols to the three Americans, she gives them weapons, instruments of death. Yet each bears her crest, the open hand holding a flower, an emblem of brotherhood, peace, life. This symbol of life later serves as a trail marker that gives the Americans the incentive to keep going toward a new life. In that life they gain a success they had not even sought.

The three Americans in turn face the three basic kinds of conflict: man against nature, man against man, and man against himself.[7] In overcoming and putting behind them each of their representative emotions, the three have won their struggles with themselves. In going to the frontier, in establishing a trading post and building it into a town, and in doing so with all the hardships and privations involved, they have won a struggle with primitive nature. As the town grows and as the three men grow old, they find themselves again in a conflict with society, just as they had been when they were trying to follow their earlier emotions. Again they must lose as they did when they were younger, and as Tallien did before them. They are superannuated, isolated.

Crawford, who does not accept this fate, struggles to the end. The other two, after Crawford's defeat, try to think about their whole history and to understand what has happened, what it has cost them, what it has been worth. Their speculation not only provides the dramatic frame for the novel but also points the reader toward the real significance of the story: the way a beautiful Frenchwoman in a warehouse in Tripoli, and in eighteenth-century France before that, caused a town to be founded on the American prairie in the nineteenth century; and she had done so merely by always choosing life.

IV *Critical Evaluation*

Harp presents individual human history expressed in stories. In such a context, the rawest American frontier town has not only its own brief history behind it but also the whole history of humanity. *Harp* is not completely successful because this true center of the novel, the flow of human history, is not directly present. The novel thus loses focus as we move from Tripoli back in time to revolutionary France and forward to the American frontier. Tallien and the Americans illustrate the futility of the three governing emotions and the irresistibility of the flow of history, but the final affirmation comes from the countess. Events of Tallien's story revolve around her, but her role has often been only passive. She is the beauty all men seek in some form, but her own affirmation of the value of the quest is insufficient because she is never fully realized as a central character. We are never made to feel the vitality of her drive for survival.

The role played in Davis's writing by his sense of the landscape is sharply illustrated in this novel. He does a craftsmanlike job of presenting both Paris and the French countryside; but, when the novel returns in the third section to the American countryside, a landscape Davis had actually seen, the change in the evocative quality of the writing is much like the change from a black and white film to one in full color. Davis has the eye of an artist, and what he has seen he evokes with descriptive writing that few writers can attain.

Davis displays considerable dramatic craftsmanship in the writing of *Harp*, also. He assembles complex threads of story and deftly handles a number of difficult time relationships. The one false note in the manipulation of time sequences is the closing of the novel at a time earlier than the one at which it was begun. This makes the conversation of Robinette and Indian Jory at the ruined trading post, the scene in which they try to understand what has happened, a dramatically false and unneeded device. Compounding such problems as overdependence on coincidence, and an incomplete time frame, the novel finally fails for lack of a clearly focused and fully realized center.

Harp is unlike any of Davis's other novels in many ways. The significance of openly historical material, the major use of foreign settings, the elaborate patterns of three, the more formal style, and the complex and incomplete switches in time are not found in any of Davis's other fiction. These features serve to demonstrate that Davis could write from his own invention and that he could go beyond the experience of his youth for material. A reader familiar with the critical reception of *Honey in the Horn* and with the tendency of critics to dismiss Davis as a "Western" writer might find in *Harp* an assertion that the Western experience is one with all human experience, or a plea for the literary respectability of the West as a subject. Whatever the reason for setting his fiction outside the Northwest, Davis gave up too much when he did. He severed the creative roots of his own experience; and, as he indicated in his journal for 1943 (126), Davis realized that a writer's creativity can do only a limited part of the work of the imagination. If the writer invents his characters, Davis wrote in his journal, the action and the moral purpose (which he assumes to be a necessary part of a story) must come from experience. If the action and moral purpose are invented, then the characters must have been people that the writer has known.

In *Harp*, Davis went too far afield from his own experience and so required too much of his creative faculty. The result is a novel that is less vivid, less intensely alive and immediate than his best writing. With its elaborately evolved triads, it is too self-consciously structured and overtly academic in its development. It demonstrates too openly and artificially what critics have often missed in Davis's best novels: that he wrote with underlying archetypal patterns clearly in mind, that the specific in his fiction is consciously and consistently related to the universal, common experience of the race. As a result, *Harp of a Thousand Strings* is Davis's least successful novel.

CHAPTER 6

Beulah Land: *Where Love Is Not Too Costly*

WITH the publication of *Beulah Land* in 1949, Davis returned permanently to the American West as the setting for his fiction, but he did not use the Pacific Northwest. Rather, he used approximately the same Southern prairie frontier area as that in which he had set the American portions of *Harp of a Thousand Strings*. Moreover, he also returns in *Beulah Land* to the journey as a basic structural element of the plot.

I The Critical Reception

The critical reception of Davis's third novel was generally favorable. Although it appeared only two years after *Harp*, reviewers ignored that work and referred back to *Honey*. The reviewers thus made *Honey* both Davis's credential as an established novelist and the standard by which they praised *Beulah Land* as a good adventure story that is comparable, and perhaps superior. Perhaps because of its quieter tone and its less obtrusive folk humor, critics regarded it as a more mature work than *Honey.* Inevitably, it was considered to be an historical novel; but it was also praised, in that context, for not seeming to be one.

Beulah Land is a more somber work than *Honey*, but there are passages in which Davis's rich frontier humor appears to lighten the tone or to suggest the irony of human events. The most often praised of the humorous passages was the account of the backwoods wedding on the bank of the Tennessee River.[1] This picture of the manners and mores of the Tennessee rural folk on such an occasion of rejoicing renewed the comparison of Davis's humor with that of Mark Twain, a comparison often made when *Honey* was published.[2] Again as with *Honey*, reviewers praised the

93

presentation of the landscape, but they felt that the characters showed little change or development from beginning to end of the novel. They noted that Davis obviously loves the land but sees the people as less than perfect. Notably, the reviewers showed none of their earlier condescension toward the Western setting, or toward the subject of frontier settlement.

II *The Story*

Beulah Land is about Ruhama Warne, a half-Cherokee and half-white girl, and Askwani, a white orphan boy reared by the Cherokees. These two are seeking an identity, a life, a place where they can live for the things they consider important. They are not so much seeking a specific physical place as they are a stable community in which they belong, but they also want a social context in which love does not cost too much.

Of Ewen Warne's other daughters, Elison, following the death of her Cherokee mother, has been reared by a white family named Cargill. She has no love for anyone but herself; and so, when her father comes to take her with him away from the hill country, she chooses the white society of the Cargills and their kind. Like them, she becomes merely a footloose opportunist who is seeking but who does not know what she seeks. Elison knows nothing about love; but her sister Ruhama loves her father and casts her lot with him wherever he has to go. At the beginning of the novel, the third daughter has not yet been born. As the daughter of Ewen Warne's second wife, Sedaya, who is also Cherokee, she will be securely Indian, and without question she will choose the Cherokees as her people and their way of life as hers.

Thus, of the three daughters of Ewen Warne, only Ruhama is caught between the two cultures and must find her way to some set of human relationships that will give her life meaning. Ruhama and her quest for her personal Beulah Land become, therefore, the center of the story.

Ewen Warne is a man without a people, a loner who focuses his life on his work, in which he finds his own identity and peace. In the mountains on the Tennessee - North Carolina border, his work is raising and marketing cattle for Crow Town, a Cherokee community in the old Cherokee Nation. When General Winfield Scott and the American army, under orders from President Andrew Jackson, come to force the Cherokees to move westward to

Oklahoma, on what was to be known as the Trail of Tears, this focus for Warne's life is destroyed.

Crow Town is not forced to move with the rest, but the circumstances are not of Crow Town's choosing. Crow Town is allowed to keep its land only at the cost of having one of its women, Sedayah Gallet, betray Cherokee fugitives to the army. The leader of this fugitive group had killed a soldier for prodding the Cherokee's wife with a bayonet as the Indians were being moved westward. When the Indian killed the guard, he fled to the hills with his wife and was followed by a few other Cherokees. Sedayah, who knew where the Indians were hiding, agreed to tell the army in exchange for a guarantee that the Crow Town Cherokees would be allowed to remain on their land. Sedayah betrayed the fugitives because of her love for the people of the village and because she knew how much they loved their land. The young Indian who killed the soldier did so because he loved his wife, and he was betrayed and shot because of love. Thus the terrible cost of love begins to appear.

The cost continues. Although Sedayah has acted as she has for them, the Crow Town Cherokees did not approve her betrayal of other Cherokees. They inflict no specific punishment on her, but their disapproval drives Sedayah to Ewen Warne. Because he at first wishes to avoid her, he decides to leave the village and his work there. When he tries to get his daughter Elison from the Cargills, so that she can go with him and with Ruhama, Elison wants to stay with the Cargills, and they wish to keep her. In the ensuing argument, Warne accidentally kills a Cargill; and, when he has to flee their revenge, he takes with him Ruhama, and Askwani. Although Warne had not planned it, Sedayah also goes with them. Their flight westward begins a chain of events that include Ewen Warne's marriage to Sedayah, his separation from Ruhama and Askwani, and the birth of Sedayah's daughter, followed soon after by Sedayah's death. Warne, Ruhama, and Askwani are then reunited and move to southern Illinois. Finally, at a cattle sale that he should not have attended, Warne is found and killed by a Cargill.

The flight of Ewen Warne from Crow Town is the beginning of Ruhama's search for Beulah Land. With her in the search is Askwani, who as a white foundling reared by Indians is as much without a people and a place as is Ruhama. His love for Ewen Warne, and later for Ruhama, is what gives focus to his search and keeps him with them. The journey of Askwani and Ruhama leads

down the Tennessee to the Mississippi, down the Mississippi to
Natchez, and then up the great river to southern Illinois. After
Warne's death, Askwani takes Ruhama and her baby sister
westward across Missouri and part of Kansas and then into the Indian Territory to the new Cherokee Nation. Finally, years later,
through the turmoil and suffering of the Civil War, Askwani and
Ruhama go northwestward to Oregon.

The long journeying of the characters gives a fascinating view of
the land and the people over a large part of America in the early
nineteenth century. We see the back country of Tennessee, Natchez
in its wilder days, southern Illinois when it was still boggy grassland
and backwoods settlements, life in the Mississippi River steamboat
commerce, early days in the prairie settlements and the Indian
Territory, and we learn some of the tricks of cardsharps and
horserace gamblers. In addition, the novel presents some little-
known aspects of the Civil War and what it meant to the Civilized
Tribes in the Indian Territory. We meet young Savacol, who has
romantically bitter poses because his mother is a whore; Perrault,
the old French gentleman who makes crooked boxes for faro
dealers; and his mistress, Maruca, a former slave who is still in love
with the memory of one of her former masters. But this variegated
view of America is only incidental to the human concerns that form
the center of the novel.

Throughout their journeying, Ruhama and Askwani learn the
kinds and the costs of love. Warne's love for his daughter Elison
leads him to kill a Cargill; and his love for his work as a cattle
herder, of which Davis reminds us as Warne helps with a calving in
Illinois (166), leads to his participation in a cattle sale and so to his
death. Sedayah's love for her people finally leads to her death (127).
Along the way, Ruhama's road is scattered with others who have
loved and who have had to pay a high price for it. When her father
is killed by a Cargill knife at the cattle sale, Ruhama reflects on the
price of love: "It was love that people were punished for hardest:
the Crow Town people for loving their land too much to do
anything but cling to it; Sedayah for loving her people more than
they were worth; old Perrault for having loved humanity when it
showed no appreciation of the favor; Maruca, for loving a dead man
too much and too long in spite of her own fear of him. . . . There
should be a place somewhere in which people could love without
being shamed or frightened or exterminated for it. There must be
such a place; it must be ahead, somewhere beyond the river,

beyond the settlements . . ." (189). This passage describes the Beulah Land that Ruhama seeks as she moves from place to place on her journey and hopes that each might be the blessed land. At Natchez, she finds she must have those she loves with her. Maruca and old Perrault are kind to her and give her a secure life, but her love is for her father, and he is not with her there. In Illinois, it appears for a time that the Warnes and Askwani have found their place in the world, but the consequences of the past again intrude in the form of a Cargill knife. Thus Ruhama and Askwani fail to find their place in white society and, at Ewen Warne's urging, they turn back to the Cherokees.

In the Cherokee Nation, Ruhama finds a tentative place that is comfortable enough, but Askwani does not. He has been physically crippled during the journey from Illinois, a journey made for love of Ewen Warne; and he is still figuratively crippled by his love for a dead man. He is still committed by this love to Ewen Warne's goal of finding Elison and to getting revenge on the Cargills. He is not free to return to Ruhama until he has met these commitments. In effect, until he is free of the effects of hate, he cannot return fully to love.

Anger at and misunderstanding of Askwani lead Ruhama to marry young Savacol, but hers is not a marriage of love, and he is incapable of any true love for anyone but himself. Their marriage is emotionally sterile, and it appropriately ends in killing, miscarriage, and Savacol's death in battle. Driven from the Cherokee Nation by the Civil War, Ruhama and Askwani, reunited after Askwani has finished his obligations to the past, finally set out for Oregon. Since settled white society and Indian society have failed them, they must finally go in search of a new land in which a new society is forming.

Before her journeys are over, love has cost Ruhama betrayal, separation, loneliness, bereavement, and sickness; but she has continued her search (286). When, years later in Oregon, Askwani is dying and Ruhama is losing her final love, she understands and accepts what she has actually found—and paid—for loving, even though it was not what she had thought she had been seeking: "Love did hurt people. It punished and maimed them sometimes, but in the end it reached down to things worth finding out, worth keeping. The important thing was to hold out to the end, to believe in love through its shifts and changes and cruelties. And the end was not an end at all, only a change. It shed and sprouted again, and went on" (312).

As he is dying, Askwani also comes to understand some of this view and to recognize that his significance as a person is finally determined by his love. He is afraid to die only because it will mean his leaving Ruhama, and he tells her on his deathbed that "There ain't anything to me except what's yours" (312). Love quite literally cripples Askwani when his foot is permanently injured, but it also saves him when, after the Northern Cherokees are driven into Kansas by Confederate troops, Ruhama finds him freezing on the prairie and takes him into her wagon. Still, after a long life together with Ruhama, Askwani is not sure their love has been worth its price to her. As he is dying, he asks Ruhama, "It wasn't what you had in mind when we started out, was it?" With her new understanding, Ruhama can only answer that it has been enough (312).

The concluding paragraphs of the novel summarize Ruhama's life after Askwani's death and give glimpses of the lives of their two daughters. One marries an Indian, goes back to reservation life, and completes in a sense the circle that Ruhama began. The other marries an Englishman and last appears in the diplomatic corps at an inaugural reception in Washington.

III   *The Basic Patterns*

Beulah Land is less dependent for its development on allusive literary or archetypal patterns than were Davis's two earlier novels. The title itself, of course, does suggest two associations that clearly fit the basic theme of the novel. Beulah Land, the land of plenty promised by God to the children of Israel through the words of the prophet Isaiah, was to be a land of peace and stability where the Israelites belonged. Although the search by Ruhama and Askwani is more for a moral and a social than for a physical place in the landscape, the two finally go together; and their search is thus associated with the whole westering movement that fills so much of the history of America.

Beulah Land was also the blessed place in Bunyan's *Pilgrim's Progress* in which Christian and the other pilgrims to the Celestial City waited, the trials of their pilgrimage over, until they were called to cross the river between the temporal and eternal to join their King. This association even more closely fits the novel because the Celestial City is as much a state of blessedness as it is a physical place. Like Bunyan's Christian, Ruhama and Askwani begin their journey as an act of love. For the sake of love, at whatever cost, they endure hardship, face challenges, and risk death; but they never abandon their pilgrimage until they find the place where they may rest secure in love until their temporal life is over.

Alternation in the novel between Indian and white civilizations suggests a comparison of the two. In the interaction of the two cultures in the lives of both Ruhama and Askwani, the possibility arises for productive new syntheses of the characteristics of both. The Indians, who have a sense of the land and love it, feel that their roots are in the land and that, as a group, they are united into a meaningful community on their common land. As a closely knit society, they conduct their relationships according to accepted customs that have been developed over a long period of time and are understood and followed by everyone in the community. Associated with this heritage, the Indians have a common set of religious beliefs.

These qualities give the Indian society a unity and stability not found in the white society that is displacing it, for the whites are restless, individualistic, and disunited. They have no respect for the land except as property from which they can make profit; and, though they have a few customs in common, they will willingly abandon them for an advantage. Since they are "on the move," neither their society nor their relationship with any piece of land has permanence; and they have no real community and so no sense of one. But, since they are capable of linear, rational thought and of linearity of purpose, their very instability has made them adept at meeting new problems and in finding new solutions.

In a world that must inevitably change, this adaptability and this ability to solve practical problems give the white society an advantage in any contest between white and red for mere practical survival. Yet without love, without a sense of humanity, without accepted custom, without mutual interest, without a feeling for one's place in both the human and the natural landscape, this practical survival of the whites leads only to cattle-trading, knife-wielding Cargills, to card-cheating Elisons, and to empty promises to allies in time of war.

What the novel suggests, then, is a synthesis of the best of both in a new land where neither is already absolutely established. The new synthesis is suggested in Ruhama in contrast with her sister and her half-sister. Her father, Ewen Warne, is a similar synthesis: he has married an Indian, and he has lived a quiet life as a herder on the land. He is clearly shown to love his work as a herdsman and to be in harmony with the essential processes of life. Yet, when his interest is aroused by a new problem, he can work on it with great diligence and creativity, and he can succeed in developing new inventions and new solutions.

Askwani also represents such a combination. Born white, reared as an Indian, fascinated by Warne's problem-solving skill, he can understand both cultures and draw upon either for his needs, just as Ruhama can. Equipped both to love and to survive in a changing world, the two represent the seeds of a new culture in a new land.

IV *Summing Up*

Davis himself liked most of *Beulah Land* better than any of his other works, but he was aware of weaknesses in it.[3] According to his journal, he tried in *Beulah Land* to give the impression of a "chronicle of reality." He wanted it to read as if the text were taken from an account of actual events. After he had finished the novel, he concluded that strict resemblance to an actual chronicle was a weakness rather than a strength. He felt instead that fiction should "try for emotions beyond the limits of actual experience."[4] Such an approach suggests that Davis belongs with those writers whom Henry James considered writers of romance, writers who deal with experience subtly liberated from "the way things happen."[5] Indeed, this practice is in harmony with his use of folklore, frontier humor, archetypal patterns, and fable. He desires to present the truth of the human heart, and this cannot always be presented merely through factual narration.

As might be expected, one price Davis had to pay for this greater sense of realism was the elimination, or at least the reduction and refinement, of his typical Western tall tales. Since Davis often uses such tales as vehicles for both humor and ironic exaggeration, the result is a much more serious and perhaps even a more dignified work. In this novel, the scenes of wild hilarity that draw comparison with Twain's humor are restricted almost entirely to the account of the backwoods wedding.

The concluding paragraphs of the novel—which quickly relate Ruhama's life after Askwani's death, give glimpses of the lives of their two daughters, and conclude with the diplomatic reception in Washington—may seem anticlimactic at first glance, but they are necessary. They help to make unmistakably clear the point of the conclusion of the novel: love does not end; it only sheds, sprouts again, and continues. As *Harp* demonstrates in another way, and with more elaborate patterns, *Beulah Land* shows that human stories never end because our lives always impinge on other lives, and those upon others still, and the effects of our actions are carried endlessly through time and around the world. What Ruhama has learned as Askwani lies dying is that love is costly because it makes each of us vulnerable to loss, but love is the best, most satisfying achievement of which our lives are capable. In the endlessness of the human story, love made infinite should be enough for whatever it may cost.

CHAPTER 7

Winds of Morning

D AVIS'S fourth and best novel, *Winds of Morning* (1952), returns not only to Oregon for its setting but also to some of the basic themes and folk patterns, dialect, and boisterous but ironic humor characteristic of *Honey in the Horn*. This novel includes an initiation story, a journey through the luminous, varied landscape and through the season of spring, an adolescent love story, and a murder mystery; but, perhaps more than in any of Davis's previous novels, the landscape helps in *Winds* to develop and reinforce the story and some of the basic patterns of meaning which underlie that story. In addition, it presents a folk history of the early settlement of Oregon, a history that is both tragic and hilarious.

I The Critical Reception

The critical reception of *Winds of Morning* was immediately favorable and was more enthusiastic than for any of Davis's previous works. Prominent critics praised it warmly. How completely *Honey* was accepted by this time is illustrated by the fact that *Winds* is praised for some of the very characteristics for which *Honey* was vigorously condemned: the magnified folk language, the irreverent humor, the eccentric characters, and the picaresque journey. The novel's commercial success was assured by its selection for the Book-of-the-Month Club.

As usual, reviewers were most often impressed with the Western setting and with Davis's presentation of the Oregon landscape. Some dismissed the plot and characters as inconsequential and reviewed the novel as a Western documentary. These reviewers made the evocation of the Oregon landscape, or such minor features as Davis's understanding of the psychology of horses, the central values of the novel.[1] Others who were most impressed by the dialect and the folk tales, called the novel "pungent Americana" and praised the "tangy" language.[2]

Fortunately, some reviewers saw beyond the Western setting and the folk materials to the central story and its human implications. A. B. Guthrie, Jr., whose own work has also had to struggle with the "Western" label, called *Winds* "a persuasive and mature work, honest to experience, wide in its embrace."[3] The usually perceptive London *Times Literary Supplement* (November 28, 1952; 173) dealt with the novel briefly but found it shrewd, humorous, and convincing. Joseph Henry Jackson, writing in the *San Francisco Chronicle* (January 13, 1952; 16, 20), offered one of the most sympathetic and perceptive reviews; for he understood that the people, not the land, were the essential focus of the work. He saw the novel as presenting people from both a pessimistic and a hopeful point of view, but the hope is hard-won after disillusioning experience.

Even these reviewers avoided the rich complexities of evolving understanding which are the real center of the work. Davis again faced the frustrating experience of being praised for the surface of his work while the substance was ignored. No notice is given to the novel's epigraph, from the Gospel according to John, "Marvel not that I said unto thee, Ye must be born again. The wind bloweth where it listeth, and thou hearest the sound thereof, but canst not tell whence it cometh, and whither it goeth: so is every one that is born of the Spirit" (3:7 - 8). Given this biblical epigraph and the obvious archetypal patterns within the novel, it is difficult to understand why even the most sympathetic critics failed to deal adequately with, or in fact even to mention, the substance of the work.

II *The Story*

Winds is the story of a young back-country deputy sheriff, Amos Clarke, and an old settler, Pap Hendricks, in Oregon in 1927.[4] Since the story is told in the first person by Amos, we see all the events through his eyes. *Winds* is the only one of Davis's novels told in the first person by a central character, and the technique gives the novel greater sharpness of focus and coherence of viewpoint.

Amos Clarke's narrative takes us through a dual initiation experience. For young Amos, it is a reverse initiation in which he moves from being a cynical young loner, convinced that human associations are usually more trouble than they are worth, to being a young man quite conventionally in love. As might be expected from such an inverted progression of attitude, his love is not that of romantic, youthful, ignorant innocence, although a kind of regained innocence is a part of it. Basically, however, his is a love that un-

derstands and accepts the risks and responsibilities that genuine
love is bound to create.

Young Amos learns much of this lesson through his part in the
parallel reverse initiation of old Pap Hendricks, an early settler in
the Oregon country who had left it years before after a quarrel with
his children. Old Hendricks has just returned not for reconciliation
with his children, but to try to achieve some of the things he felt
that he had missed doing in the early days. These missed
achievements are never specified, but the progress of Hendricks's
initiation is marked by his developing acceptance of the fact that he
can never go back to his earlier possibilities. He has to face the fact
that during those early years in which he was trying to "get a
start"—in effect, trying to get ready to live the life that he had en-
visioned for himself—he was actually in the process of living. For
better or for worse, that had been life. As a result of this latter-day
initiation, old Hendricks arrives at a new understanding of the consequences of genuine love and at a new acceptance of the responsibilities that love creates.

Besides being a double initiation story, *Winds* is also a murder
mystery. Although the solution of the mystery is not the central concern of the story, the solution does help to lead both Amos and Hendricks to their new understanding of themselves and their
obligations toward life. Amos first becomes involved in this chain of
events when a ranch foreman named Sylvester Busick unintentionally kills an old Indian, Piute Charlie. Amos arrests Busick as
much to get him clear of the angry Indians as to take him to jail;
but, as they travel toward town, Busick proposes a detour across the
river to tell his boss what has happened. By doing so, he hopes to
get the boss's lawyers to arrange his release so he can avoid a night
in jail. Since the river is the state line, Amos fears that, once across
it, Busick will not return with him. For this reason, he refuses, and
gives Busick a grudge against him.

When Busick is tried on a charge of manslaughter, the Indian
women who witnessed the shooting are bribed to lie, and the jury is
rigged because Busick owes money to a number of people in town
whom he could not pay if he were in prison. The lying of the
women and the acquittal by the jury publicly discredit Amos and
imply that his testimony had been perjured. Had Amos suspected
such tricks, he might have prevented or exposed them. He does not
learn of them in time to stop them because, just at the time the
defense case is being presented, Busick's daughter, Calanthe, comes

to the sheriff's office and keeps Amos there in conversation. Amos is for a time not sure whether or not she had been a knowing part of the scheme to discredit him, but he later concludes that she was not.

As a part of the financial "settlement" under which Busick is acquitted, he relinquishes his title to a herd of horses being tended by old Hendricks. With Busick out of jail and bearing a grudge against Amos, the sheriff wants to get Amos out of town for a while to avoid trouble. As a way to do so without making Amos appear to be running away, the sheriff assigns him to finding Hendricks and the horses. Once he has found him, Amos is to help Hendricks move the horses to open range in the higher back country.

The sheriff had not been available to make the Busick arrest because he was investigating the murder of a wealthy rancher named Farrand, who had been shot by a member of a railroad track gang. The only witness to the murder was Farrand's wife, who claimed after the shooting that the track worker had intended to rape her. During Busick's trial, Amos has helped in the search for the track worker, and so he is involved in the effort to solve that murder.

When Amos finds Hendricks and the horse herd, the old man is being helped by a young Mexican named Estéban d'Andreas. The three of them set out on horseback on the arduous task of moving the horses through wheat country to open range. This task puts the central events of the novel into the context of a journey on horseback through eastern Oregon in the early spring. As the drive progresses, Hendricks finds himself called upon repeatedly to help various people: Busick's daughter Calanthe, a youngster named Asbill whom Estéban shoots when Asbill tries to steal some of the horses, and Estéban himself when he is put in jail as a vagrant. Hendricks recognizes Asbill as a grandson, although he does not reveal the realationship to the boy; and he learns that the Farrand widow is one of his daughters. She, too, appears to need help, but at first Hendricks resists seeing her. These episodes delay and lengthen the journey and give old Hendricks occasion to tell Amos tales of the early settlement of the country. In these stories the people have lived their lives according to their "sentiments," in spite of what it may have cost them in wealth, comfort, and peace of mind.

Events and some detective work finally lead Amos to realize that their companion and helper, Estéban, is the man who shot Farrand; he is the "murderer" whom the whole countryside is seeking, but Amos and Hendricks know Estéban to be a gentle, timid man who is unlikely to have committed the crime as it was described by Farrand's widow. Just as they make this discovery about Estéban's crime, they encounter Calanthe, who has overheard conversations between Mrs. Farrand and Busick, whom the widow has inexplicably hired to be her foreman. From those conversations she has learned that Busick knows something about the murder and that he has used his knowledge to blackmail Mrs. Farrand into hiring him. Moreover, Calanthe believes that Busick may force his advantage to the point of marrying Mrs. Farrand. Disgusted by this perversion of what she believes love should be, Calanthe has run away from her father.

When Hendricks learns of this relation between Busick and Mrs. Farrand, he finally accepts full responsibility for his past and decides that he must talk to his daughter, from whom he hopes to get the full truth about the murder and about Estéban's role in it. He has resisted such an interview because this is the daughter who had been responsible years before for driving him from the country. When she was thirteen, Hendricks had gotten into a dispute with his grown children over the sale of his property. His wife had died, most of his children were grown, but this daughter, who was still at home, had sided with the other children and had run away from home. When Hendricks had caught her and brought her back, she had charged that he had tried to rape her. Rather than fight such a charge and continue the quarrel with his children, Hendricks had left the country. His decision to talk to Mrs. Farrand represents, therefore, his full acceptance of the responsibilities of love. She had been his favorite child, and he realizes that his love for her goes even beyond the wrong she has done to him. By learning the full truth about the killing of Farrand, Hendricks may save his daughter both from doing further wrong to Estéban and from an unhappy and evil life under the domination of Busick.

The interview clears up the mystery of the murder of Farrand. Estéban had indeed shot him, but only because Mrs. Farrand had filled him with lurid and untrue stories of Farrand's brutality to her. She had invented these stories only because she hated her husband and the life she was leading with him. Believing these stories, Estéban had come upon a situation that he misunderstood; and Mrs. Farrand had encouraged his misunderstanding. From a distance, Busick had seen enough of the shooting to know that Mrs. Farrand's account to the sheriff had been untrue. This knowledge had given him the opportunity to blackmail his way into a foreman's job and perhaps into marriage and ownership of the Farrand ranch.

Without revealing all of his reasons for doing so, Hendricks persuades his daughter to drive Busick away, at whatever risk of exposure. He is able to do so because he convinces her that he still loves her, that a father's love must reach beyond any wrong that can be done to him. He, in turn, accepts responsibility for Estéban, who is, in a sense, also a victim of the killing of Farrand. Although morally Estéban is innocent of any wrong intent, he is still legally guilty of the murder, and would surely be hanged if turned over to the sheriff.

With the murder of Farrand solved and with Busick's hold on Mrs. Farrand broken, Hendricks, Amos, and Estéban complete the horse drive. Hendricks and Estéban prepare to settle into a life of horse-herding in the high country. But Hendricks has not yet supplied all of the pieces to the puzzle about his motivation. At an abandoned pioneer graveyard, Hendricks searches out the grave of his wife, and there he confesses to Amos what his real sin had been, what had actually led to alienation from his children and to his acceptance of exile. In an unusually hard winter on a high-country homestead, Hendricks and the other settlers had run out of feed for their cattle and had been about to lose them to starvation. There was unused grass on the Indian reservation, but no way to lease it from the Indians. To gain access to that grass, and so save his cattle and his homestead, Hendricks had taken an Indian woman as his mistress. She had gotten him access to the grass, and his cattle had been saved. The affair had meant nothing more to Hendricks than survival of the homestead, but it had so deeply hurt his wife that she was thereafter completely alienated from him. In succeeding years, she had turned more and more inward until, by the time she died, she had been living in a private, secret world of her own.

With this acknowledgment of the wrong he had done his wife, Hendricks now appears to be at peace with his past and to be settled into the beginning of a new life. After Amos's assigned task of taking Hendricks and the horses to open range seems to be completed, he accordingly prepares to return to his life in town and to a search for Calanthe. But Busick appears. Having been driven off of the Farrand ranch, he is ready to kill Amos and Hendricks so that he can use Estéban to renew his blackmail of Mrs. Farrand. Estéban stops him by shooting him in the shoulder, the third shooting this gentle young man has been forced to commit. As he is doctoring

Busick's wound, Hendricks tells Amos the final piece in the puzzle of Hendricks's actions, a relationship of which neither Busick nor Mrs. Farrand has known. Busick is Hendricks's son, Mrs. Farrand's half brother; for he is the child of the affair with the Indian woman. With this revelation, Hendricks takes responsibility for Busick as a third member of his horse-herding enterprise. In this final act that occurs on the site of his original sin, Hendricks rises to his full moral stature. Here he shows Amos that no one can avoid the consequences of his past acts: each must accept his own past and his children's future.[5]

All of Hendricks's past is now accounted for, and he can settle into his new responsibilities. He sends Amos to search for Calanthe and to begin his own new life. Amos's search symbolically takes him back toward town, back from his isolation to rejoin human society. He acknowledges this fact through successive requests to various groups of people for information about Calanthe. He returns finally to Hendricks's first horse camp near town, the place from which his journey through spring had begun. There, as the winds blow away the petals of spring to make room for the promise of summer, Amos finds Calanthe; and the cycle of love begins again.

III   *The Basic Patterns*

In the Western experience of settling new lands, Davis continued to find the Eden story a useful pattern for interpreting the human predicament. In *Honey,* the Adam-figure is the youth, Clay Calvert; and, in *Winds,* which is set nearly two generations later in the late 1920s, the Adam-figure is the old man, the original settler, Pap Hendricks. The youth, Amos Clarke, who belongs to a later, postlapsarian generation, is involved in the consequences of the sins that lost Eden and created the need for the atonement of Christ, the second Adam.

Amos's name introduces the second biblical theme that Davis uses in this novel, for the prophet Amos had prophesied doom for Israel because of its transgressions. Amos, although much younger than Hendricks, is the more cynical and worldly wise of the two; and he is fully aware of the sins of the inheritors of Canaan. This Amos, like the prophet of the Old Testament, is also capable of a concluding affirmation of at least limited and provisional hope for Israel. For Amos Clarke, however, the affirmation can come only after his initiation into a new meaning of innocence.

At the outset, we see Amos as a sheriff's deputy: a prophet, a deputy of the Lord, bringing the word of the law to the people. The outcome of the court case against Sylvester Busick—acquittal so that Busick can pay his debts—is exactly the first offense of Israel that the prophet Amos names: "They sold the righteous for silver" (2:6). To arrive at such a verdict, the jury has had to imply that Amos's testimony against Busick was a lie, thereby committing another offense which the prophet names: "They hate him that rebuketh in the gate [court of law], and they abhor him that speaketh uprightly" (5:10). Parallels in the novel to other offenses named by the prophet can be worked out, but those just mentioned are the most direct and should be sufficient to indicate that Davis intended to arouse such biblical echoes in *Winds*.

What the latter-day Amos learns, however, is that the line between righteousness and evil is neither so clear nor so simply identified as he first believes. As Amos first learns of Busick's acquittal, Davis introduces the image of a desert water hole (44 ff.). Simply passing the pool reveals only surface reflections of the land and sky around it. When a traveler stops to drink from the water, he sees below the surface to the teeming, complex life beneath. The rest of Amos's experience in the novel becomes a process of looking beneath the surface of the community, of coming to understand, and finally of accepting the life he finds there.

For Amos Clarke, the cynic crying corruption, the journey with the Adamic Hendricks back through spring, back through the morning of the race, back through Canaan to the scene of the original Eden, is an initiation. Amos begins by crying corruption; but finally, with full knowledge of the evils and errors of mankind, he is able to act out of affirmation and hope, just as did his namesake at the end of his prophecies. The people of Israel, the prophet concluded, "shall build the waste cities, and inhabit them; and they shall plant vineyards, and drink the wine thereof; they shall also make gardens, and eat the fruit of them. And I will plant them upon their land, and they shall no more be pulled up out of their land which I have given them, saith the Lord thy God" (9:14 - 15). After the desolation of lost hopes and abandoned homesteads through which Amos and old Hendricks travel, such a promise would indeed be an affirmation of a better future for the people.

The biblical associations of old Hendricks with Adam and Christ are more complex and more essential to the development of the novel. Even so, they are intended to be allusive, not strictly allegorical; they awaken echoes of the whole history of mankind and show once again that the human story goes on eternally. Old Hendricks's life is not revealed strictly chronologically but through successive depths of significance as Amos gazes ever deeper into this pool of life. The story of his relationship with the Indian woman and the hurt it caused his wife is not revealed until nearly the end of the novel, for example. The logic of this sequence is the logic of the pool, rather than of chronology or of suspense mystery. The revelations come as Amos penetrates successively deeper into Hendricks's personal history and motivation.

These successive layers of Hendricks's past make the full reasons behind Hendricks's behavior as much a mystery to be unraveled as the real facts behind the killing of Farrand, although the focus is not on mystery as such, but on Amos and Hendricks. Taken chronologically, the story of Hendricks as an original settler begins with the Lilith story in Eden and ends with the atonement of Christ, the second Adam, for the sins of the first. Lilith, a figure that appears in the mythology of a number of the civilizations of the Middle East, is in Jewish tradition Adam's other wife, the one suggested by the first of the two accounts of the Creation in Genesis. She was the one created simultaneously with Adam ("male and female created he them," Genesis, 1:27); however, she was soon expelled from Eden because of her pride and was exiled to the regions of the air. Her exile gave occasion for the creation of Eve from Adam's rib, as related in the second chapter of Genesis.

In Arabic mythology, Lilith married the Devil and became the mother of evil spirits. Her name derives from the Sumerian word for "wind"; but, in Hebrew, her name is also associated with a bird, the owl.[6] In the story of Hendricks, the Indian woman becomes a Lilith because she comes between Hendricks and his rightful wife and causes the wife's alienation. From his relationship with the Indian woman comes the feeling of guilt that drives Hendricks from the country when his children band against him. To emphasize the Lilith parallel, already hinted in the "wind" association of the title, Hendricks's wife in the later days of her life draws birds that had "come into her mind" (319). Since the Indian woman also bears Busick, who has the role of an evil spirit in the novel, the wind-spirit Lilith is at least a part of the wind that sweeps away the Eden in the morning of settlement in Oregon.

As might be expected of Adam, Hendricks acknowledges that he has children "littered all over" the country (19), but at first he is willing to condemn his children to Hell (64), to do nothing to save them. The low point in his attitude toward life in that country comes when he sees the ruins of the Waymark place, an abandoned homestead. After telling Amos the story of that family and hearing how it had ended, Hendricks exclaims that Waymark had been cheated, and that he had put more into life than he had gotten out of it. In these early passages, Henricks shows signs of giving up the purposes for which he has returned. He is in danger of falling into a disillusionment even deeper than Amos's.

Yet Hendricks does not forget that he has returned to Oregon to try a new start in the country from which he had earlier been driven. To fulfill the biblical pattern that has been suggested, however, the character of Pap Hendricks must become Christlike. This quality is first suggested early, when Hendricks knows, or imagines, more detail about the Farrand shooting than an ordinary human might be expected to know from the information given. As he is revealing this knowledge, steam from the coffee bucket makes "a sort of veil before his face" (75).

As the journey with spring to ever higher country continues, Hendricks assumes more and more responsibility for helping others. He concludes that he must look after his own, even if they are worthless, even if he does it only for "sentiment" (95). When he and Amos help Calanthe pull her truck out of the spring mud, Hendricks even hints at some responsibility for Busick by telling Calanthe that all Busick owes him for his help is good behavior (120). Yet, even as he more and more takes responsibility for helping others, Hendricks still conceals some deeper trouble, some dread; and Davis associates this fear with the advancement of spring (143). Such a coupling of spring life with dreaded atonement again suggests Christ.

Hendricks's progress toward resolution of this unknown dread leads him to make increasing commitments to helping his kin and, at the same time, produces further manifestations of supernatural power. While he is in Crosskeys to help his grandson, young Asbill, he meets Amos in a darkened stable and shows him that he can see in the darkness (190 - 93), a supernatural ability Davis gave to Godlike Dee Radford in his short story, "The Homestead Orchard." This new sign of unusual perception is followed by a reversal of his statement of despair at the Waymark place. In Crosskeys, Hendricks concludes that "what a man gits out of life don't count for a damn in the long run. It ain't what you git out, it's what you put in

that lasts. Some of it lasts as long as you live, and maybe after
you're dead, and it's the only thing that will" (198).

That the problem is one of love is made clear even while Hendricks is still refusing to take the ultimate step of responsibility and
go to see his widowed daughter (228). Finally, when he learns that
Busick and Mrs. Farrand may marry, he resolves to face the final
trial that he has tried to avoid, the final responsibility that he has
sought the whole time to ignore: he decides to go to South Junction
to see his daughter.

Hendricks announces his decision in mockingly religious terms,
but those terms have a deeper, serious meaning. When he says that
he has been "redeemed and transfigured" and that he has "felt the
witness" (248), he is in effect announcing the atonement that is to
come. He recognizes that it is an atonement that must be made
(249); and, from this point onward to the conclusion and the aftermath of his interview with his daughter, the association with the
crucifixion of Christ is made increasingly apparent.

To reach South Junction, Amos and Hendricks and Estéban have
to swim the horse herd across the river, a crossing that is made difficult by the high waters from melting mountain snows. In the
midst of the crossing, Hendricks is accidentally struck on the head
and knocked from his horse into the river. As a symbolic wounding
and baptism, this scene begins the series of images that associate
Hendricks with Christ. These images are carried out to their symbolic conclusion in Hendricks's interview with his daughter; for, at
the outset of that interview, Davis makes a point of telling us that
Hendricks is sitting under a beam that has a hook and a pulley on
its end. "It was intended for hanging beef to be dressed, but it did
look considerably like a gallows" (291). Davis also calls our attention to Hendricks's wound: "The bump on his head where the
driftwood had tagged him looked painful, but he paid no attention
to it" (291). As a parallel to Christ's crown of thorns, Hendricks's
driftwood-wounded head suggests that the crucifixion is near.
Finally, on the same page, Hendricks refers to another of his
daughters, Euphemia, as willing to "help stretch a man out to be
crucified. . . ." In helping to arrange the meeting between Hendricks and Mrs. Farrand, Euphemia has done exactly that.

The interview with his daughter amounts to a crucifixion for
Hendricks, but his triumph comes with his final realization of the
boundlessness of his love for her. The resurrection that comes from
this atonement is the rebirth of the sense and meaning of love

within both Hendricks and Mrs. Farrand. The daughter tries to find the limits of his love, as if to go beyond them and escape the obligations of love; but Hendricks refuses to set any (300). His unlimited love brings her to tears and to an agreement to drive out the demon Busick: "it was the consciousness of being loved that had finally started her crying: not guilt or remorse or fear, but being made to see how far she had fallen short of what she had been loved for to begin with: the failure, the waste, the desecration" (307).

The cost of this conversion for Hendricks is the crucifixion and figurative death of his former self, from which he must arise to his final assumption of responsibility for others. At the end of the interview, he looks "white and old." He takes his daughter back to her house; and, as he does so, there is "a dead sound to everything that was said, like after a burying. . ." (305). Appropriately, it is on the third day after this scene of atonement at South Junction that Hendricks completes the pattern of love and responsibility by assuming responsibility for Busick and thereby full responsibility for all the sins of the past. The pattern of atonement and rebirth is then complete. Both Hendricks, the Christlike figure, and Busick, the Satanic figure, are disabled and are being served by Estéban "because they had attempted more than they were equal to" (334).

Estéban d'Andreas's name suggests in Christian context both Stephen, the first martyr, and Andrew, one of the disciples. In Estéban's unwilling compulsion by events, in his passive acceptance, and in his devotion to Hendricks, these names add appropriately to the Christian pattern. The final piece of this pattern of sin and redemption, Lilith and Eve, love and atonement, comes years later. Amos reports that, after old Hendricks is dead, his two charges, Estéban and Busick, go their separate ways. Busick, true to his demonic nature, "drifted down into the mining country. . ." (336).

IV   *Love and Isolation*

Another pattern of significance to the development of the novel is the interplay of loneliness and love. Both Amos and old Hendricks are alone at the beginning, isolated from society: Hendricks, by his guilt and rejection of his children; Amos, by his prophetlike vision of the corruption of humanity. Amos at first accepts his loneliness as he rolls up in a borrowed blanket to sleep in the haymow of the livery stable: "It was lonely, but having too little company beat hell

out of having too much. There had been lonely people up the river
and none of them appeared to mind it: the section boss, the skinny
girl hanging out her wash by the camp wagon, the Hasslers on their
woodscow, Pap Hendricks in his horse camp; even Piute Charlie"
(26). We learn, however, that Amos is wrong about both Calanthe
and Pap Hendricks; they do mind loneliness.

Amos even transfers to the landscape this desire for simplicity
through isolation. When he is riding alone into Crosskeys, he is (or
pretends to himself to be) glad that Hendricks is not with him to
associate the landscape with the affairs of people: "It was a kind of
deliverance to spread down beside the old orchard without knowing
who had set it out or what his character had been or what sentiments he had squandered his life's enthusiasm on" (154; see also
152 - 53). Despite all his resistance, Amos cannot escape the human
pull of friendship. When he comes on rock lilies in bloom, he wishes
for company: "There was a kind of empty feeling about looking at
them alone. There was such a thing as seeing them too many times,
with only the same things to think about them all over again. Two
people looking at them together might have scared up something
new to think about them" (158). Even as he is riding into Crosskeys
he feels it: "I had ridden into it against the lights in the dusk more
times than were worth counting up, though never before without
wishing that some sleight-of-hand operation could turn it into
something different for a change—Constantinople or Alexandria,
maybe. . . . Old Hendricks made it more worth coming back to,
seemingly" (180).

Calanthe, from her loneliness, finally makes Amos face the meaning of his, and the fact that he would prefer not to be alone. In the
scene with the playful pack horse (252 - 56), she brings the subject
into the open and forces Amos to face it. From that point it is clear
that his loneliness will end with her, and hers with him; but he also
has much to learn about love. As Hendricks has told him, "Love can
hurt like hell" (87); but Amos does not fully learn the lesson until
he sees what love has cost the old man. Along the way to that final
knowledge, the stories of other early pioneers, the Waymarks and
the Powells, prepare him to understand.

The series of three dreams that Amos has about Calanthe at intervals in the novel obscurely but intriguingly foreshadow the yet unknown relationship between Hendricks and Calanthe (grandfather-
granddaughter) and the developing love between Calanthe and
Amos. In addition, the dreams are a deftly handled device by which
Davis keeps the developing love of the two young people before us

and believable in spite of the fact that Amos and Calanthe actually see very little of each other during the novel. Amos's first dream, which is part of a longer, complex reverie-turned-dream, begins with scenes from the Oregon landscape. Next comes a reflection on the change from the early days of settlement, when nature was the enemy and people were given more value, to Amos's time, when nature is a refuge and people must be feared. This dream is followed by comical scenes of petty human foolishness.

As Amos dozes, his conscious mind lets go and his subconscious takes over. As this happens, the ironic scenes run together and fade, to be replaced by a scene with Calanthe much like the one on the hillside in which she made clear what she intends their relationship to be. Amos sees the dream scene as an opposite to the scenes before, and therefore as some indefinite kind of affirmation. The only action in the scene is Calanthe asking an unheard question and then releasing a small, dark bird from her hand (274 - 75). Amos makes nothing of the dream, but the total context of the novel gives the bird ambiguous meanings. On the one hand, the tiny bird released in the bright sunlight suggests the beginning of their love and of Amos's rejoining humanity. On the other hand, the fact that Calanthe is the granddaughter of the Lilith of the story suggests that, through her association with Amos, Calanthe can rid herself of the Lilith association and stay with him in the bright sunlight.

The second dream again involves a bird, again with an ambiguously negative possibility (310). Amos sees Calanthe running along a sunlit ridge, but she is running in a shadow like that of a bird overhead. It is not clear to Amos whether she is trying to avoid the shadow or to stay within it. He does not yet know that Calanthe is the granddaughter of the Indian woman, but the dream suggests to the reader that Calanthe is still in the shadow of her descent from the mythologically winged spirit of Lilith.

In the third dream, Amos sees a fire burning the straw of wheat harvest, but the sunlight is so bright that he cannot see the flame. Calanthe comes and casts a shadow on the flame with her hand, making the flame visible, seeming to give the straw a hand of fire (339 - 40). Thus the shadow of Calanthe makes the fires of harvest visible to Amos. The fire that burns the straw clears the ground for a new planting, just as, in the end of the novel, the winds of morning blow away the "wreckage" of spring, the problems and mistakes and disappointments of the early settling, to make way for a new beginning in a summer season.

Davis uses dreams not only to foreshadow for the reader what is to come in the story but also to establish Amos's preoccupation with Calanthe, despite his denials. They force Amos to recognize that he cannot evade the question of his relationship with Calanthe: "As with the two earlier dreams about her, there was no meaning to it, but it settled one thing. It would be useless to send anybody else to tell her about her father. I had to see her myself. It was the only way to keep some vague uneasiness of conscience from dogging me with meaningless dreams at night" (340).

V *The Uses of Folklore*

Davis made heavy use of the materials of folklore in most of his fiction, but he did not always integrate it fully into his story in his earlier work. For this reason, the folk material has been criticized as extraneous and distracting, however entertaining it might be in itself. This criticism is undoubtedly the basis for some of the more supercilious and superficial dismissals of Davis's work as that of a local colorist. By the time he wrote *Winds*, however, Davis had full control of the folk materials and made them an integral, essential part of the work. In *Winds*, he uses folk speech, folk tales, and superstitions both structurally and thematically in the development of the story.[7]

The colorful folk speech serves a number of purposes for Davis. Most obviously it makes the reading lively, entertaining, colorful, and often amusing. Although the folk expressions are certainly more artfully used and more frequent than would have been the case in reality, they provide a sense of verisimilitude, a sense that we are experiencing the talk of real people in a specific place at a particular time. Folk expressions also permit the injection of a wry irony that Davis uses to attain distance between the writer and the ultimate seriousness of his subject. Through the use of irony, the indirection and understatement so characteristic of such folk speech, Davis also can characterize individuals in his story. The brash, youthful cynicism of Amos Clarke emerges clearly in such speech. In the same way, such witty vernacular establishes the vigor and clarity of old Hendricks's mind and helps show that even at his most serious he is neither pompous nor self-deluding.

The anecdotal use of folk tales in Davis's other novels has been criticized as digression and failure of focus. Sometimes this has been true, but in *Winds* Davis's use of such tales is not a structural interruption but an effective device for moving the story forward. For example, the story of the Waymarks provides the occasion for old Hendricks's first, and lowest, evaluation of what life has been for his generation of early settlers.

What people put into life, Davis shows us in the folk tales, is based not on hard practicalities and calculations but on their "sentiments," their aspirations and illusions and affections. Thus the story of the Powells, full of jealousy and murder and loneliness (91 - 95), and the story of Clallum Jake's lifelong gratitude to the Kirkbrides (134 - 35) show the basic motive forces, the human emotions, that move the people to behave as they do. These forces finally affect Hendricks and Amos and the outcome of the novel. The Powell story also illustrates the human preference for love over isolation, and the price humans will pay for love. Hendricks suggests that love is the motivation in the Powell story, but Amos shows by his cynical response that he has not yet learned the power of love.

Other tales are used to help develop the theme and consequences of loneliness, isolation, and the need for human associations for a meaningful life. The herder who tries to conquer loneliness by teaching magpies to talk but finally has to kill them (185), the two Welshmen who refuse to depend on or be obligated to anyone else (259 - 60), and the Ryczek family, who refuse to share meadow land with the Indians and also refuse to use normal channels of society for justice (258), are all steps in developing the futility of deliberately choosing isolation as a way of life.

Folk tales that parallel the patterns of the central narrative generalize that story into the stream of universal human experience. They suggest that individual lives work themselves out as a part of the great flow of history. The triumphs or failures of any single story contribute only a very small ripple to the stream of history, sometimes making individual lives seem to be of little consequence. Demonstrating the unimportance of such lives can have two effects: on the one hand, it makes the ironic, mock-heroic humor of Davis a vehicle for presenting stories dwarfed by the inevitable tide of events; on the other, it gives the individual story a wry dignity by showing that it represents a common experience of mankind.[8]

VI   *Illusion and Reality*

The history of the West has been a history of interplay between illusion and reality. The West has been seen as Eldorado and as the Great American Desert, as a howling wilderness full of savage

followers of Satan, and as the new Garden of Eden where mankind
has another chance for paradise on earth. The settling of the West
has been the story of successive encounters between these various illusions and the realities of the region. The drama and suspense of
that settlement have come largely from the ways in which the
settlers have dealt with the differences between their expectations
and the realities they have encountered. The contrast between expectation and reality is one of Davis's continuing themes and a principal aspect of *Winds*.

When Pap Hendricks settled in Oregon, he hoped that it was a
new Eden in which there need be no fall of mankind. The past had
no meaning; he looked only to the future, to his hopes for his
children. But the West was not Eden; or, if it was, the settlers
brought the serpent with them when they came. Hendricks himself
commits the sin that brings alienation and dissolution of his hopes
for earthly paradise. When his children fail to live up to what he
had expected them to be, they show in their turn the presence of
the "marplot of Eden."

How Hendricks responds to this clash between illusion and reality, expectation and result, forms the ground of the novel. His first
response has been flight, complete abdication of responsibility, but
this action has taken place before the time in the novel. We first see
Hendricks when, for vague and perhaps not consciously realized
reasons, he has returned to the scene of his failed Eden. Even with
his return, he appears unwilling to face the full force of the failure
of his illusions. He clings to the early Edenic illusion that "all the
stretch" has not yet been worked out of the Oregon country, that he
can start again on much the same terms as he did the first time. He
will not see his children. He will in effect pretend that he has learned nothing from his earlier failures.

This effort fails. At the Waymark place, when Hendricks concludes that Waymark was cheated, that he had put more into life
than it had given him, Hendricks is proposing complete abandon-
ment of illusion for the harshest kind of reality, but he cannot long
sustain this position. When the drip in the attic of an abandoned
building calls to mind the story of the Powells, Amos tries to dismiss
it as a sound with natural causes, and he offers to find them. When
Hendricks replies that he would prefer to keep the illusion, he establishes the tension between illusion and reality that he must
resolve, if he is to come to terms with his own past life and find
meaning for his present and future life.

The epigraph for the novel, taken from Saint John, speaks of rebirth of the spirit. For Hendricks, this rebirth, which is associated with the images of Christ and the crucifixion, becomes a reconciliation between illusion and reality. Hope and idealism are easily sustained when the new settler sees the land and the people in the light of optimistic illusions. Hope and idealism for what can yet be attained become more difficult, but more noble, when confronted with full understanding of reality. To continue to aim higher than can ever be attained, and to know that the aim is impossible, is not so much perverse insistence on illusion as an affirmation of Hendricks's conclusion that what we put into life is more important than what we get out of it. He believes that the spirit of man can transcend the harsh realities of the material world. Man's body cannot escape its mortality, but his spirit can rise above that reality and live by its "sentiments" despite the pressures of reality. But reality cannot be ignored in the West, any more than human sentiments can be discarded. To come to fruitful terms with the promise and disappointments of the West, Hendricks and those like him must have a rebirth through the spirit; they must find a way to face reality without abandoning the ideal.

VII   *The Affirmation of Nature*

The rebirth of every spring after the death of each preceding winter presents a background for this continuing affirmation of the vitality of the human spirit. Hendricks and Amos travel continually through the first stages of spring as they work their way to the high country. From the low point of despair at the Waymark homestead, Amos looks back and sees "all the dead tangle of plum twigs in the thicket around the burned house had started to put out white blossoms. Anybody would have taken oath twelve hours earlier that they were all dead" (143).

Repeatedly, as they travel past the wreckage of abandoned homesteads, they see that nature is healing its scars and bringing its own life back: "It was consoling to think that nature could take hold of an orchard that had been planted as an outpost against the wilderness, and, with scarcely an effort, turn it into a wilderness itself. . ." (154). Grass seed presses through the drying adobe that a man could hardly break with a pick. All through the men's journey the seeds sprout, the birds nest again, the flowers bloom, a little locust blooms through a crack in a board sidewalk in Crosskeys

(225). Nature is a healer, a force to life in the face of whatever destruction.

Contrary to the early days when nature was a threat to the survival of the first settlements, nature has become a haven, a reference point, a source of continual renewal. With the means of survival of human life assured, nature had become "the great healer: the hydrophobia skunk that had been turned into a household pet by sterilization and surgery where it would do the most good" (272). Some day, Amos realizes, humanity may manage the same transformation from the enemy of life to the affirmer and creator of life. Nature has become for him a refuge from evil, and some day humanity will undergo the same transfiguration: people will become "restorers of peace and faith . . . God's first temples . . ." (272).

Amos, the experienced cynic, knows that such a time is not near; for he does not blink at the worst in humanity. He gives us a graphic contrast between nature and the sordid evil of which man is capable when he takes us to the rigged crap game in the railroad station (205 - 13), nor can we miss the contrast between that scene ("the stench of railroad disinfectant; the clutch of floor dust and dried spittle; the weak old light bulb frying scum from dirty hands on its hot glass; the players' faces like moldy bread, their eyes fixed like gouts of cold slime; a girl like that in the middle of it working as a capper for the shoddiest specimen among the whole pack of them, the filthiest, and having a good time at it" [212]) and Amos's relief on going from that scene into the cold night air: "the sharp air and distant sounds, and the coarse grass underfoot, and the smell of damp greasewood and juniper in the wind. . ." (213). Even so, because nature reminds Amos of the possibilities for healing and peace and faith, he is willing to continue to have hope in spite of man's failings.

VIII   *The Artistic Achievement*

To an extent, *Winds* returns to the picaresque pattern of *Honey in the Horn,* but *Winds* is more tightly structured and more clearly linear in its development. In *Honey,* as we have seen, Davis takes Huck Finn to the West and helps him find a satisfactory conclusion to his search for a place in the world. In *Winds,* he gives us both a Huck Finn (Amos) and a Don Quixote (Hendricks); for Amos, like Huck, is an isolated boy who has prematurely seen so much of the evil of the world that he thinks he does not want to belong to society. Old Hendricks is full of ideals and illusions that are old fashioned and much too pure and exalted for any possible realization in this imperfect world. Both figures are absurd, heroic, and tragic; but Davis, unlike either Twain or Cervantes, finds a resolution to their dilemma that permits them to keep their ideals, and even some of their illusions, and still live effectively in a real world with normal human society.[9]

The combination of the journey of discovery of both an idealistic old man and a cynical youth gives the story a dual focus on what the past has been and, as a result, what the future may yet become in the West.[10] The conclusion of the journey expands and qualifies but also validates to an extent the vision of both. The quixotic idealist must learn that life is now, not in the future, and that ideals have consequences and will exact a price. The cynical realist must learn that people do indeed live by their sentiments, and that the style of their lives—what they put into them—is finally what counts.

The major themes of all of Davis's previous novels can be found in some form in *Winds*. Like *Honey*, *Winds* presents the adolescent question of isolation versus membership in society, and it concludes in favor of society. The intermeshed continuity of all human history and the irresistibility of its movements are here as they are in *Harp*, and so are the basic emotions of love, vengeance, and ambition. The kinds and the costs of love, and the values that make those costs acceptable, are presented in *Beulah Land* and appear again in similar terms in *Winds*. Thus Davis's fiction becomes more complex, his themes more richly interlocked, and his control of his materials more complete in this, his finest novel.

CHAPTER 8

The Distant Music

D AVIS'S fifth and last published novel, *The Distant Music,* is a condensed family saga that presents the history of the Mulock family, how they came to settle in Oregon, and what that settlement meant to succeeding generations.[1] In his earlier novels, Davis made an individual consciousness the center of the story and moved that consciousness through the countryside on a journey. In this novel, Davis sets a family homestead as a center and moves the reader through time, the time of three generations of Mulocks, whose lives are tied to that homestead. Although Davis deals with themes touched upon in his earlier novels, he does so through a reversal of his earlier, picaresque pattern.

The none too complimentary picture of The Dalles that Davis presents in "A Town in Eastern Oregon"[2] attracted considerable attention and of course raised the hackles of the hometown folk, but Davis was never completely satisfied with it. In his introductory note to *Team Bells Woke Me,* Davis suggests that the sketch is all right as far as it goes but that it does not go far enough to have fully presented his subject: "What is needed is not more material, but a more deeply-studied thesis" (xii). Because Davis recognized that "some flicker of deeper truth" had not been reached,[3] he presents in *The Distant Music* some deeper truths about Oregon: what happened to the hopes of the first settlers and to the generations that followed.

I   *The Critical Reception*

The Distant Music is not a pleasant novel. It lacks the frequent boisterous, if usually wry, humor of Davis's most successful works; and this characteristic was often noted by reviewers when the novel was published. In view of the tendency of most reviewers to miss the real point of Davis's writing, it should not be surprising that the somber tone produced negative reactions. Davis's masterful presentation of the Oregon landscape, however, continued to draw such praise from reviewers that the landscape overshadowed the plot and character in their reviews. The novel was considered to be rambling and lacking in focus,[4] more concerned with the land than with the people,[5] but worthy of praise for its "sustained, melodious passages of description."[6] The novel was criticized for the absence of the picaresque qualities characteristic of many of Davis's earlier novels; but, like these novels, it was still considered to be weak in plot and to lack dramatic impact.

Some reviewers did see that Davis was exploring not only the relationship between the people and the land but also what possession of the land had meant through the generations after the first settlement. What matters to Davis, one reviewer wrote, "is the homely, tragicomic dance of humans in Nature's beautiful madhouse."[7] Generally, reviewers ignored the title and the significance of it that is suggested by the novel's epigraph, taken from Marco Polo's *Travels*.

The most perceptive and laudatory review was written by another Western writer, Walter Van Tilburg Clark.[8] Clark noted the connection between *Distant Music* and "A Town in Eastern Oregon," and he suggested that Davis had at last gone after that "flicker" of deeper truth and had found it. Clark recognizes the importance of the land as the "motionless center" of the novel. All motion in the novel, he notes, radiates outward from the land and is drawn back to it, and the central characters' movement away from their land decreases as the novel progresses. What this cyclical, diminishing motion finally shows, Clark concludes, is the helplessness of the individuals in the face of their situation, their predicament, their fate.

Comparing this novel with Davis's other novels, Clark recognizes that in trading the journey for the unmoving land, Davis is simply showing us the other side of the coin of experience with settlement of the Pacific Northwest. As early as *Honey*, Davis makes Clay Calvert realize that the settlers were, as Clark says, "migratory herd creatures who find themselves best in company and in motion." When they settle down, as they do in *The Distant Music*, they begin to "entertain such homemade illusions as Progress, Betterment, and Civic Virtue." When that happens, they begin, in some way, to resemble Davis's town in Eastern Oregon, with all its self-defeating pieties and reforms.

II *The Story*

Of the three generations of the Mulock family who lived in Oregon from the time of early settlement to the twentieth century, the first of the line is "a set-mouthed man . . . named Ransom Mulock."[9] This first Ranse Mulock comes from Missouri and shows a great deal of the stubborn skepticism traditionally attributed to natives of that state. When Mulock arrives at Clark's Landing, a small town on the Columbia River, with a herd of starving, footsore cattle he has bought from an Indian village and driven across the desert, he nurses the cattle to health, fattens them, and then sells them. With this money he returns to the Indian village and buys freedom for a white girl, Medora Crawford, whom the Indians two years before had found abandoned after the disintegration of a wagon train lost in the mountains. After Rance marries Medora, he takes her to Clark's Landing; and he immediately files for two sections of riverfront land for homesteading, twice the amount he could have claimed had he remained single. This advantage of his marriage leaves in the minds of the people of Clark's Landing the impression that Ransom had married Medora only to get more land—and Ranse and Medora acknowledge to each other that this view of their marriage is correct.

After a desperately hard trip across the desert, the Mulocks are camped on their land in only a crude shelter in bitterly cold weather, when Medora has the miscarriage of a child fathered by a Blackfoot Indian from the village in which she had been held. At just that time, three men from Clark's Landing come visiting to see if Ranse really is entitled to file for a married couple's homestead. Because they recognize what is happening to Medora, the situation becomes common knowledge in the town. Ranse resents the people of the town for their malicious inquisitiveness and is driven by a desire to accomplish more than they think he can. To do so, he is constantly involved in work that takes him away from home, packing, freighting, acting as guide, dealing in livestock, or doing whatever offers hope of economic gain. He uses some of his first money from these enterprises to buy lumber and begin a big house on his land, but he remains so busy that he only builds the framework and completes a few habitable rooms on the ground floor. The house stays in this state through the whole novel, a symbol of an uncompleted dream.

Medora bears Ranse two sons, Claiburn and Ransom. She has

remained sympathetic to the Indians and therefor is helped by squaws in the birth of her second son, who is born while Ranse is absent on business up the river. While on a steamboat, Ranse encounters the Indian by whom Medora had conceived the child that had miscarried. The Indian, identified by a small mirror he wears on a string around his neck, is drunk and is insolently doing a mocking, obscene dance on the steamboat in front of a group of army officers' wives. When Ranse shoots him without warning, the second shot shatters the mirror. Ranse then jumps off the steamboat, swims ashore, sets out for home afoot, but is found dead two or three days later from a heart attack.

With the first Ransom Mulock's death, the long bondage of the family to the land begins, as does his family's failing struggle to keep the land intact. When Medora sells some land to a railroad to obtain money to get a Blackfoot Indian out of jail, her older son, Claiburn, leaves home, becomes a trouble-making wanderer, and finally is killed. Although he seems to have desired to escape the hold of the land, he actually has left because Medora has sold some of it. In this way, his departure and his later death result from the family's bondage to the land. The second Ransom stays home, tied to the land; and, when Medora dies soon after Claib's death, Ranse assumes the struggle to hold the land.

Ranse becomes involved with Old Inman, an itinerant carpenter and a building contractor who talks Ranse into subdividing some of the Mulock land, building houses on it, and selling the property on time payment plans to railroad and factory workers. Ranse also gets acquainted with the Inman children: Isom, the grown son, Pickett and Dell, the younger sons; and the three daughters, Tencey (Hortense), Cynthia, and Lydia. Ranse, on an impulse, almost casually marries Stella, an outcast girl from the town. She bears him a son, the third Ransom Mulock; but she soon thereafter runs away with Isom, and the Inman family begins to break up. The girls marry and move away; the father finally leaves, but, as usual, he leaves his building project incomplete. Faced with financial disaster and loss of the land, the second Ranse pulls himself out of the illness and the constant drinking into which he had retreated when Stella left him, and runs his property. He finally leaves the old house, moves into one of the larger of his tract houses, and spends his years managing his property and rearing his son. He reminds himself from time to time of his vow someday to leave Clark's Landing, but he never does so.

When in his fifties and feeling like an old man, Ranse again encounters Cynthia Inman, who is now a widow with a grown
daughter. When he invites her to be his housekeeper, he does not
know that his son is in love with Cynthia's daughter, and that his
son and Cynthia's daughter have quarreled. When Ranse tells his
son that Cynthia is coming to live with them, young Ranse, fearing
that Cynthia's daughter will also live with them, quarrels with his
father and threatens to leave if Cynthia does move in. When his
father insists, young Ranse leaves home and temporarily escapes
from the land and works on the railroad.

Nina, Cynthia's daughter, does not move to Ranse's house, but
Cynthia's two sisters, Tencey and Lydia, who are also widowed, do
so. This grouping gives Davis an opportunity to contrast the lives of
these three women, who have not been tied for life to a single piece
of land, with that of the second Ranse Mulock, who has been. At the
age of sixty, ill, feeling old, Ranse finally attempts at least a symbolic escape from his land: he walks away from the house when the
sisters are not aware that he is leaving and he wanders along the
bank of the river that crosses his land. While searching for old
Ranse, Lydia finds young Ranse on a work train in the railroad
yards and enlists him in the search. Old Ranse, who is finally found,
has had a slight stroke, has suffered exhaustion, and has been
beaten and hidden by young thieves who hope to get a reward for
finding him. As he is returned to his house, he believes he is dying.

Since the search brings young Rance and Nina together, they are
reunited; and it becomes clear that young Ranse will now stay on
the land, manage the property, and marry Nina. Old Ranse, as he
prepares for what he believes is his death, asks Lydia to tell him
about the world away from Clark's Landing, the world he has missed. As she does so, Lydia realizes that her life, although full of suffering and losses and disappointments, has been far better than the
Mulock life of bondage to a place. With this realization by Lydia,
the novel ends.

III *The Basic Patterns*

The meaningful patterns of this novel grow from its title, *The
Distant Music*, and from the epigraph from Marco Polo's *Travels*,
from which the title is taken:

This desert is the abode of many evil spirits, which amuse travellers to
their destruction with the most extraordinary illusions. . . . Sometimes

during the day these spirits assume the appearance of travelling companions, who address them by name and endeavor to conduct them out of the proper road. Marvellous and almost passing belief are the stories related of these spirits of the desert, which are said at times to fill the air with the sounds of all kinds of musical instruments, and also of drums and the clash of arms.

The first Ransom Mulock had crossed the desert, and he had also continued throughout his life to hear the distant music of illusion. His name suggests both his character and his role in the settlement of the West: "Mulock" indicates the unsociable stubbornness with which he gained and held to the land while avoiding any relationship with the people of the town of Clark's Landing. This stubborn immovability, like the name, survives through the three generations of the family. "Ransom" is exactly what the first of the line began for both Medora, the mother of the line, and for the land on which they lived. The parallel between Medora and the land, which is persistent throughout the novel, helps to unite the structure of the novel around Davis's central theme. Both Medora and the land were originally possessed by the Indians, and neither is ever fully free from the Indians, even after having been "ransomed" from them by Mulock.

The Indian union with the land, like the union with Medora, becomes finally a sterile one, ending with a miscarriage. Regardless of romantic notions to the contrary, the novel suggests that, in both cases, the Indian view of their relationship with the land and with Medora went no deeper than desire for immediate gratification. In his antics on the riverboat, Medora's Blackfoot Indian lover exhibits such an attitude toward women; and his view about the land is suggested by the fact that he is returning from a "treaty conference" in Portland, "glowing from the flattering unction of being whipsawed out of some more of their tribal lands, heavily conscious of their dignity and importance, and in some cases not entirely sober" (73 - 74). Both the land and Medora can be "bought" from the Indians; both can be ransomed for a price; but an ambivalence remains about whether the real captivity is before or after the ransom.

Neither Medora nor land was what Ranse was seeking when he went west, but they were what he found (206 - 207). Once he found them, he held to them and forgot what he had originally sought. The land, and in a sense Medora, become a trap for Ranse, and each holds him to something he had not intended. Furthermore, since neither Medora nor the land is what Ranse thinks each is when he first attains them, he feels that he has been betrayed. The betrayal imagery begins with Medora's dream (31 - 34, 42) that Ranse has been stabbed in the back by the Blackfoot father of her miscarried child; and this sense of betrayal remains with Ranse throughout their years together until he kills the Blackfoot. Ironically, the lifting of this burden of betrayal brings about Ranse's death; he cannot outlive his betrayal—and his final days indicate that his burden had kept him alive.

Medora, like the land, is relatively static; but Ranse moves, wanders, dreams, and then returns to Medora. Even in the matter of a house, the two are different. Ranse dreams about a mansion, buys the lumber, makes a beginning, but never finishes it; Medora wants only a little cabin, a practical dwelling for immediate comfort and not for show. This union of dream and reality, movement and stability, uneasy though it may be, ends only with the first Ranse's death. In succeeding generations, the Mulocks will be static because of the promises exacted by Medora as she is dying. For the other element, the movement and the dream, Davis introduces the Inmans; and they contrast with the second Ranse who is completely static. Old Inman, who is completely rootless, moves from place to place; he is always building and arranging and projecting; but he never completes his projects nor realizes whatever his dream has been. By the second generation, Davis has split movement and stability into two streams in which movement is associated with dreams and illusions; stability, with retreat and stagnation.

Illusion has been introduced early with the first association with Medora and with the land. The wagon train from which she was lost had broken up when it became stranded in unnamed and unexpected mountains, for its people had followed tracks that led nowhere. As the situation became desperate, the people of the train had mistaken a snowcovered mountain range for the spires and gables of a village. After a wet snow had put out their fires (in a situation suggesting "Kettle of Fire," soon to be written), the settlers had mistaken steam from a hot spring for a fire in the hills and had wanted to send some of the youngsters "to find out what it was and bring back a kettle of coals" (150). In her dying delirium, Medora returns not to reality but to these illusions, holding fast at the last to the final illusion that the land was what all the suffering and sacrifice had been for.

If the elder Inman represented the restless dreamer that is eternally "in man," his daughters carry this sorting of life styles even further. Tencey, the oldest and a teller of tall tales, enjoys embroidering on experience; and, when she makes it more colorful and exciting than the reality, she has given her narrative the dramatic essence of the folk tale. The early instances of her yarn spinning are clearly for amusement, to tease the second Ranse (127 ff.); but, in her later years, her tale telling is an ingrained reaction to life. With Ranse bloody, unconscious, and apparently near death, she launches into a story about the attempted suicide of a man at Tin Pot, but Cynthia stops her (285).

Tencey's life with her husband had been one of dances and parties and jokes and fun that had been supported by the progressive selling of portions of the husband's farm, until her husband died and the children sued to save what land was left. "Tencey had no regrets over having frittered so much valuable property away on nothing . . . there would have been no pleasure in going on with the frittering all by herself. It was watching her husband at it that she had liked. The pleasure he took in it kept her from realizing what foolishness it was, and, looking back, she couldn't help feeling that it had been worth it" (208 - 209).

Cynthia, on the other hand, is the one most like the townspeople of Clark's Landing: she lacks the depth or the imagination to have significant illusions or to hear distant music: "the plump unlined face, the wide-open gray eyes that saw everything on the same plane, all the deeps and shallows as shallow, all the small incidents and big ones as big, the mind that could call back hurt and horror and waste and a loose window-sash that needed fixing in the same patiently tragic tone . . ." (190 - 91). It is especially fitting that Cynthia is the one to keep house for the second Ranse when he begins to feel that he is old, and it is right that she is the mother of Nina, because Nina is the practical woman who extracts from the third Ranse the promise that he will return and care for the property.

Lydia, the third sister, is the one with moral depth; she seeks a balance between movement and stasis, between destructive illusion and sterile lack of imagination. She has been the stabilizing influence in the Inman family, the one before whom solemn promises are made, the one who tells Ranse the real truth after Tencey's tall tales. Yet Lydia has not remained static; she has traveled, lived, suffered. She has seen the mirages on the desert and has learned that the mirage looks different to each person who sees it, because each has seen it as himself (302). Thus Lydia understands the nature of the illusion and the price of following it; and she is the one character who finally speaks for Davis and gives us the conclusion to which the novel leads.

The third Ransom Mulock tries to escape, but he cannot because his ties to his father and to Cynthia's daughter, Nina, are too strong. Perhaps of equal importance is the fact that he has no unexplored, desert landscape in which he can seek to hear the distant music of illusion or to see the mirage that is finally only his magnified self. When he flees the land, he can only work for the railroad, just as when his father tries too late to escape, he gets no farther than a view of the railroad yards. The third Ransom must accept defeat (279) and continue to pay for the land that neither he nor his father has really ever wanted.

After Medora, the irony of the bondage lies in the slow yielding of the land to the town. The untouched, undeveloped beach land has a harsh beauty and an austere purity that is lost as the land is "developed." The second Ranse realizes that the "Land that had been graded and dug up . . . could never be the same. . . . What had been lost stayed lost" (160). As the captivity on the land becomes tighter, the land becomes merely tract houses and industrial sites. Finally, the land even keeps the second Ranse from full human relationships. This is made apparent when he cannot allow Stella to have power over it (168), and he is reserved with widowed Cynthia for the same reason (196). The land has isolated him not only from humanity, but finally from himself (206). Even as he realizes his situation, Ranse understands that the land had not been what Medora or any of her dead had wanted: "The land was not what they had given their lives for. It was merely what had got tangled in the net they had thrown out for other things, probably better and certainly different, that had escape it" (207).

If this story of the Mulocks and their land had ended with the final entrapment of the third Ranse by his promise to Nina that he will stay, the novel would have had a grimly negative conclusion. However, in the closing scenes Davis shifts the focus from the Mulocks to Lydia. Lydia's presence and her account of the country away from Clark's Landing give the second Ranse the will to continue to live. Although Lydia provides the only real escape from the family land that the second Ranse will have, her account finally leads her to find her own conclusion about the value and significance of their lives.

The perception of Lydia as being in some sense the successor to the perception of Medora is suggested in the parallel reveries that lead to emotional "seizures." These episodes come as the full accumulation of the cost of life crowds in on the consciousness of each woman. The first comes with Medora's dream of the Indian who stabs Ranse in the back. The second dream is precipitated not by news of Ranse's death, but by news of his shooting the Blackfoot and her realization of how long Ranse had carried that pain. The third seizure comes for Medora after Claiburn's death, and this one kills her. As her life is praised by speechmakers at the dedication of the new railroad, "some memory in her of what her hardships and sacrifices had really amounted to and what they had done to her" is finally more than she can bear (120).

A similar crowding of memories strikes Lydia; for, exhausted by her search for Ranse, she finds herself weeping uncontrollably. When she is overcome by "regret for lives that cost so much struggle and anxiety to preserve and returned so little for it" (256), the basic tension of unresolved regret in Medora's life is transferred to Lydia for ultimate resolution. Faced with the failure of old Ranse to die when he has decided to do so, she is confronted by people from Clark's Landing who have come to congratulate old Ranse for surviving. Given their shallowness, she at first sees the prospect of his survival as pitiful. Significantly, it is Tencey, the teller of tall tales, the purveyor of illusions, who tells Lydia one more tale, about a man who had come west with their father's wagon train.

Like old Ranse, the man had reached a point at which he wanted to give up his life as of no further value. Yet the other men from the wagon train kept him from doing so. Life, they said, meant too much for them to allow anyone to throw it away. This final affirmation Lydia reaches for all of them, whether they are held motionless by the land or lured ever onward into the desert by illusion. "If they were right, the places she had lived and left behind and all the lives she had touched and lost had not been wasted, and nothing of all she had gathered was either dead or useless" (311). What Lydia's net had caught had been life.

IV   *Critical Evaluation*

The Distant Music fits the patterns of Davis's other novels more consistently than is at first apparent. In abandoning the picaresque technique of showing us the people of the West in motion, Davis is only showing us the same people in a specific place while the land changes around them. He still shows us people working out their destinies in the context of the broad, richly evoked Western landscape of Oregon. He still adds depth and, although this is generally a somber novel, some humor, through folk tale and country humor. And at the base, his conclusions are still the same as those he had reached regularly in his other novels: Humanity cannot live a meaningful life on the basis of things or possessions, whether they be land or money or cattle or any other tangible form of wealth and power. Hendricks in *Winds* concludes that what a man puts into life is more important and satisfying than what he gets out of it. Early in this novel Ranse Mulock thinks that "what a man had . . . counted, not what he had done" (41); but he learns immediately "how dead and meaningless a man's gains could seem when some implement he had used to acquire them fell apart in his hand" (42). Although Lydia does not articulate her view so clearly, she at the last agrees with Hendricks.

This contrast between those *having* (the Mulocks on the land) and those *doing* (the Inmans, ultimately Lydia with her losses) serves to demonstrate the necessity for a balance between reality and illusion. Illusion that never comes to terms with reality can create old Inman or his son, Isom, who ends in desperation with murder and suicide. Reality without illusion can lead to the sterility of the Mulocks. Lydia, the balance, has been on the desert and has seen the mirage, but she has also known the depths of pain and terror and understands their part in life. She has known these as the price of touching other lives, of loving and giving, not of seeking and demanding. Like Ruhama of *Beulah Land*, she has learned the cost of love.

The Distant Music contains some deeply moving scenes and, as always with Davis, some brilliantly evocative descriptions of the landscape; but, as a whole, it is not a successful novel. The scope of the novel—three generations of a family as well as seven or eight of the most crucial decades in the settlement of Oregon—is too great for adequate treatment within a work of only slightly more than three hundred pages. The resulting compression of events does not permit adequate preparation for or presentation of the key scenes and the crucial actions.

In Davis's earlier novels, the point of view is carefully controlled and consistent. In *The Distant Music*, this tight consistency breaks down, and the fully omniscient author takes over. This loosens the presentation of the story and creates a need for compensating structural tightness that the novel does not achieve. However, the most serious structural difficulty is the shift in point of view at the close of the novel from the Mulocks to Lydia. For the middle generation of Mulocks, Lydia has functioned much like a Greek chorus; she has observed the antics of both Mulocks and Inmans with a clear, realistic gaze; and at times she has kept them honest by her mere presence. But we have always seen her from Ranse's viewpoint, until her final search for Ranse. From that point, we shift between Lydia and the young Ranse until we reach Lydia's recital of the places she has seen and the experiences she has had as she talks old Ranse back to life. From there we move to the conclusion in Lydia's mind, the solution of a tension in her view of her life.

This shift is a weakness because until the closing scenes we are not concerned with any tension in Lydia's view of life. We have focussed on the tensions of the Mulocks who have been struggling to escape the bondage of the land, to hear again the distant music of illusion that will lure them into either physical or spiritual journeys. From this viewpoint, the novel ends in failure because Lydia's resolution to this struggle does not touch the Mulocks. The author actually provides the resolution; but he finally does not convincingly dramatize it in the novel.

The extreme compression of events gives the reader the sense of reading an outline of what might become a family saga, perhaps a trilogy. The fact that the novel was published in 1957, the year following Davis's loss of a leg to arteriosclerosis, suggests that Davis may not have been able to focus his full critical powers on the completion of his novel. In good health, Davis might have expanded the novel to a length that would have permitted full treatment of a subject of such scope. Since no concrete evidence exists that this was the case, our explanation is the merest speculation. But, after the artistic mastery of *Winds of Morning*, the failures of *The Distant Music* are especially puzzling if no such cause can be assigned.

CHAPTER 9

The Achievement of H. L. Davis

H. L. Davis is one of a few recent writers who have re-
claimed the West and the frontier experience for American
literature. Ultraromanticized stereotypes that had no relationship
with the actual Western experience had so dominated the popular
concept of the West by the 1930s that serious literary treatment of
the region was neither recognized nor accepted for its real artistic
merits. The result of this almost automatic stereotyping was the
removal of the American Western experience from the range of subjects available to serious imaginative artists in this country.

Ironically, this exclusion occurred at least partially because the
drama of the exploration and settlement of the West has so
dominated the American popular imagination. Mass-media ex-
ploiters of popular tastes pounced upon the West and reduced it to
the formulas of dime novels, pulp magazines, and "horse-opera"
motion pictures before serious artists could establish its genuine imaginative potential. With this major part of our national history and
cultural context rendered unusable by the dominance of facile but
instantly hackneyed convention, our serious literature for some
decades of the late nineteenth and early twentieth centuries was
restricted to the East and the South, but some occasional grudging
admission of the Midwest occurred. The result was a serious distortion in our literature of the American experience, a distortion from
which our arts, and our critics, have not yet entirely recovered.

A major accomplishment of H. L. Davis, along with a handful of
other writers, has been to reclaim the Western experience for real
artistic exploration. Davis, as well as such writers as Walter Van
Tilburg Clark, Harvey Fergusson, Wallace Stegner, and Frank
Waters, ran the risks and accepted the penalties imposed by the
Literary Establishment on those who seek to deal seriously with the
American West. Examination of the critical reception of Davis's
novels suggests the kind of price such authors have paid for writing

134

out of their own cultural heritage and experience, but their courage and persistence have begun to reopen this rich vein of essential American material for serious literary treatment. In a very useful pioneering study of some of these writers, F. E. Hodgins has concluded that Davis was one of the new writers about the West who "have recreated in imagination a part of our American heritage that was lost to fiction" and that, in doing so, he added a new depth and complexity to American literature.[1] Of this group of Western writers, Thomas Hornsby Ferril in 1960 called Davis "probably the most important writer of the modern West."[2]

Davis's West is not the West of a new frontier; it is not a promised land in which superhuman heroes perform superhuman feats. It is another setting in which the eternal human experience of love and hope and ambition, as well as betrayal and disappointment and defeat, can be acted out. This West offers the writer some dramatic advantages over older sections of the country; for, new and open, this region is a stage upon which these patterns occur with a directness and clarity not so easily found in an older, established, stratified society. On a frontier, particularly, the issues can genuinely be life and death, not merely the life or death of a social position or of a political career. This stripping of life to its essential elements can lead to the exploitation of easy effects for sensationalism, but used properly it can give the serious artist's work force and directness. Writers such as Ernest Hemingway and Joseph Conrad have amply demonstrated this principle by using African, Asian, and European settings; and the experiences of their characters suggest that the Western experience is at bottom one with all human experience.

The West that is central to Davis's work, however, is the West into which he was born in the last decade of the nineteenth century and, more important, the West of his childhood and early adolescence. As Wallace Stegner has suggested, there is a period sometime between the ages of five and twelve when the child receives impressions that govern his perception of the world for the rest of his life.[3] For Davis, that critical period in his childhood came after the real frontier had closed; and it was a time for reality, a time of abandoned homesteads and shattered dreams. The mass enthusiasm and hope of the Great Migration to Oregon was gone. A few of the dreams and some memory of the glory survived among the old-timers who had lived through the frontier days, but the young people saw only the reality of hard times without a new fron-

tier to which they could flee. They knew that the land was neither
Eden nor Eldorado, that there was no gold in the hills, and that rain
does not follow the plow. They had learned that Western farmers
and ranchers were even more at the mercy of transportation and
marketing than their fathers had been in the East.

At this point of balance between the old dreams and the new
realizations, Davis brings into ironic play this conflict between the
old and the new, not to glorify one and discredit the other, but to
seek a usable balance between idealism and cynicism, between unrealizable dreams and passive acceptance of the status quo. Davis is
too clear eyed to continue to follow the old, outworn dreams of the
West; but he will not deny the human spirit the right to dream. The
resolution of this tension between cynicism and idealism is the central force in most of his fiction.

Such a resolution clearly is not simple and cannot rely on formulas and stereotypes. Instead, Davis approaches the problem
much as Amos Clarke describes looking at a desert waterhole in
Winds of Morning: a glance may reveal only surface reflections, but
a closer look shows rich layers of life beneath that surface. Davis
uses the same technique on the life of rural Oregon: he takes us
close to the surface and helps us to see, in the pool, "a whole new
world as active and populous as your own, different from anything
in it and still part of it" (44). Strange perhaps, different certainly,
but still full of life, it is a part of our world.

I *Style*

Davis was a writer of considerable originality and flexibility. He
did not write by formula or set pattern. On the other hand, most of
Davis's work is related in some organic way with the whole body of
his writing. Each of his novels, for example, builds in theme, style,
structure, and other ways upon those that have gone before. Given
this unity of development in Davis's writing, a few technical aspects
of his work that deserve particular consideration are style, structural
techniques, the uses of folklore, and the uses of the landscape.

Davis's literary style is characteristic yet supple and adaptable to
a variety of purposes. Perhaps most characteristic is Davis's use of
vernacular both in dialogue and in narrative. Although this vernacular is clearly the heightened product of conscious artistry, it is
based on folk expressions and therefore gives an air of verisimilitude—of indigenous reality and immediacy—to his work.

A characteristic of such Western vernacular is its ever-present underlying vein of ironic humor. It is rooted in the masculine Western tradition of offhanded stoicism and understatement in the face of a harsh life and frequent danger. Strong emotions are usually concealed, or revealed only partially and indirectly, in this style. The implicit humor usually present also allows Davis to write scenes highly charged with emotion and human tragedy without becoming sentimental in the presentation. Such humor does create at times an air of aloofness, a sense of philosophical detachment that makes some critics uneasy. However, this sense of olympian noninvolvement is only on the surface; it is a device that allows the reader to supply the emotional reaction rather than forcing him to accept the author's. As in Western humor, understatement can sometimes be more powerful than the most explicit and direct statement when presenting pathos or tragedy.

When Davis switches from dialogue and narrative to description, he uses a different prose style—one that drops the aloof indirection and ironic humor and looks instead directly at the thing described. When Davis is describing landscape, the reader is reminded that this writer began as a poet. Commenting on this obvious connection between Davis the poet and Davis the novelist, Carl Sandburg wrote, "As a novelist he can't stay away from streaking in a poem regularly without labeling it as such."[4] Davis of course was quite aware of this aspect of his style, and he employed it deliberately for his own artistic purposes. Some three years before Sandburg's comment, Davis acknowledged in a letter to Thomas Hornsby Ferril that "The novel, even at its best, sneaks poetry over on [the reader] by disguising it as information."[5]

The disguise is easy to effect because of Davis's poetic style, which is itself underplayed. Davis does not give us his reaction to the landscape through evaluative adjectives: he presents the landscape itself. He tells us the colors, the sounds, and the smells; he gives us the names of the flowers and the feel of the wind; he shows us the lay of the land. The descriptive detail is both profuse and precise, and by involving all of the senses, Davis increases the impression of profusion by pressing in on the reader's perceptions by all possible avenues. This is the effect of Davis's technique of praising by naming.

The contrasting tones of these variations in style provide one useful mode for the presentation of Davis's story. The language itself suggests that in the affairs of humanity there are choices, decisions, consciously considered alternatives available to the actors. These make the characters capable of creating profound emotional impact by having choices be either grand or ridiculous, or both. The landscape, on the other hand, has no capacity for irony or choice; it is what it is, inexorably. Its beauty is there only if perceived by either a character or the reader directly through the writer's voice. Its beauty finally can be only in the eye of the beholder, but the way it is perceived by a character becomes a part of that characterization. Presented directly by the writer to the reader, it becomes a context, a stage which lends its presence as a commentary on the way the actors play their parts in relation to it.

II   *Structural Techniques*

As a sophisticated artist, Davis used a number of structural techniques in his fiction, such as manipulation of the point of view, multiple flashbacks, grouping of narrated events into patterns, allusive use of archetypal patterns, and so on. Although many of these have been discussed in some detail in the examination of specific works in earlier chapters, two are so characteristic and pervasive in Davis's fiction that they merit general comment in any attempt to summarize or to evaluate Davis's literary achievement. These are the use of the picaresque journey as a central dramatic device and the use of contrasting pairs in a constant counterpoint around a central theme.

The journey as the basic dramatic structure of a novel or short story is a device often and successfully used by Davis. Unlike the traditional *pícaro*, however, Davis's protagonists parallel their physical journey with development of perception and understanding. The people and situations they have encountered along the way become more than mere focuses of incident and excitement: they become steps along the road to some final awareness or resolution for the protagonist. To serve such a function, events must be anything but random adventures. They must be carefully selected and structured, for each person or incident must fulfill a particular role in the story's development. Clay Calvert, for example, must have a number of experiences and learn a number of intermediate lessons about love and guilt before he is ready to face and accept Luce's guilt and his own. He must learn and accept a lot about the nature of humanity, good and bad, before he is ready to join society. Both Amos Clarke and old Hendricks must travel through a specific series of problems and choices before Hendricks can re-unite his present with his past and before Amos can move to an af-firmative future. The physical motion provides a dramatic line along which the development of the characters occurs.

Another common structural device for Davis might be called the technique of counterpoint.[6] In this Davis uses alternating, opposing, or complementary pairs: idealist and cynic, age and youth, isolation and society, Indian and white, past and present, illusion and reality, movement and stasis. Often these contrasts provide not only the motive tension of the plot but also illustrate the contradictions of life in the West. Davis's complex view of life keeps these contrasts from becoming polarized at extremes, and the resolution of tension between them generally arrives at some middle ground. His counterpoint never presents purely black and white absolutes, but a basis for interaction and development. Such counterpoint especially fits both the times and the topics with which Davis deals in most of his fiction. His time was a point of balance in the West between the old dreams and the new realizations of reality. Davis brings into play this conflict between the old and the new not to glorify one or to discredit the other, but to seek a usable balance between idealism and cynicism, between unrealizable dreams and the passive accep-tance of stagnation.

III   *Folklore*

Like Hawthorne, Twain, Faulkner, and other major American authors, Davis has used folklore as a basis for significant art. The way Davis employs folk materials in his work is perhaps one of his most artful techniques, but it appears as one of the most artless. Because of some of the regional characteristics on the surface of the folk materials Davis has used, many readers have, ironically, missed the universal elements common to most folklore. Moreover, Davis uses folk materials in a variety of ways. As he observes in *Harp of a Thousand Strings*, "the stories of a land are the cumulative assertion of what it is, its character, its people, its individuality, its being" (266). In this way, folk tales give a sense of place and of a people. They provide not only richness of context for Davis's principal story line but also rhythm for the progression of the story through il-lustrative diversions. These tales throw sidelights on the story, il-lustrate the central themes, and expose the common elements of human experience in them.

Critics have frequently cited Davis's use of folk tales as an aspect of his Realism, but such usage is not their primary function. Davis has noted that his unsentimental treatment of the West has often been praised for its faithfulness to life, to "the real thing." To Davis, such an objective is only the means to a more significant effect, for "A book should do more than catch life as it is. It should widen the reader's understanding of the possibilities of life and its meaning, whether missed or attained. . . ."[7] This heightened revelation of the possibilities of life suggests, on the one hand, the "possible other case" of Henry James and, on the other, the artful exaggeration of the tall tale. This combination, the essence of Davis's use of folk tales, introduces the element of romance into the work with the very material for which Davis is praised as a Realist.

This paradox is resolved if the true nature of folk tales is properly understood. The stories do indeed grow out of the real experiences of real people, but the tales themselves are not simple, unembellished, factual accounts of actual events. If they were, they would merely be oral history, not tales. What these tales do, in their gradual evolution from a basis in experience, is distill the central elements of the common experience of the folk into a representative story. Part of what makes such stories representative, however, is the addition of judicious heightening. Real life seldom has the clarity, the ironic humor, or the concentration of folk tales that represent the possibilities of the race, not the actual experience of some single individual. Although Davis's tales are never sentimental, they are romantic in the best sense since they present the possibilities of human experience in ways that seldom actually occur but that are true to the human heart.

IV   The Landscape

The aspect of Davis's writing most often mentioned, and most consistently praised, is his presentation of the natural landscape, particularly when it is that of Oregon. This evocation of the scene represents both a skillful avoidance of a number of common pitfalls for Western writers and a useful technique in the development of Davis's fiction. The hazards faced by the serious writer in presenting the Western landscape have been well analyzed by Thomas Hornsby Ferril, who speaks of a "low-grade mysticism" that is encouraged by the scope and the grandeur of Western scenery. To Ferril, "The imagination, transported by enormous mountains, deserts, and canyons, endeavors to answer landscape directly and tends to disregard, or curiously modify, what might otherwise be normal considerations of human experience," even though that experience gives the landscape meaning. This distortion of the creative imagination by the Western landscape, in turn, tempts the writer to people that landscape with "men to match my mountains," supermen who become stereotyped heroes.[8]

With the exception of a few scenes on the Columbia River and on the deserts in eastern Oregon, Davis avoids most of this problem by presenting only the immediate landscape in specific detail. He does not use grandiose panoramic pictures, for he usually presents the flowers blooming in a mountain meadow without expanding the view to the whole mountain or to the range of which it is a part. Since Davis most frequently presents his landscapes as they are perceived by one or more of his characters, he focuses on how the character is affected by the landscape, rather than on the landscape itself.

These characters generally see the landscape as a stage for the awesome continuity of the life force in both plants and animals. The coyote kills the sheep and is killed in turn. When the snow comes and covers both, the mice clean their bones under the snow. By spring, all traces of death are gone. Blossoms appear from the most gnarled and apparently lifeless wood. The irresistible cycles of nature continue quietly, regularly, in spite of the human comedy and tragedy for which they provide the setting.

Nature was an important part of Davis's writing even in his earliest poetry. It provided various symbolic associations: a river or a white bird for wildness; the sexuality of a spring, of tall, straight poplars, or of hills "in foal" with ripening grain. The cycles of the seasons, of gardening, or of farming provide patterns that suggest the seasons of life: the time of year and the weather often set the moods and establish the backgrounds of human emotions and actions. The constancy of nature and its inevitable cycles often contrast to the ephemeral affairs of humanity. The landscape thereby becomes a metaphor for the inner landscape of the people and for their sense of a passing or a passed life.

Because of the inexorable, invariable, nonemotional procession of the life processes in nature, Davis is able to make dramatic use of the landscape in his fiction as an offset, or foil, or illustrative contrast to the human dramas played in the broad natural setting. In musical terms, we might regard the landscape as the continuo over which the characters play out their individual human melodies. In his early novels, Davis often only used the landscape as a colorfully varied background to go with the varying events of the journeys; but, with the mature mastery shown in *Winds of Morning*, Davis integrates the landscape fully into the development of the novel in much the same way as he had earlier in such short stories as "Open Winter" and "Homestead Orchard." In *Winds*, the coming of spring becomes a continuing affirmation that people are finally able to achieve. In this fashion, the landscape becomes a norm, an unwavering constant of continuity and unequivocal life force against which we may measure the whims and vagaries of the human scene, just as the continuo provides the basic chords within which the melodies of life must all be played.

Since Davis's writing was a part of the development of his own view of life and of humanity, his works represent a part of the process of solving problems, of gaining broader understanding, of resolving tensions, and of coming to conclusions. As his principal characters arrive at acceptance of some aspect of their lives, their solution most likely represents a similar acceptance for Davis; for an artist's emotional maturation must surely be reflected in that of his art. In this connection, it is interesting to note that the most prominent season in Davis's poetry is autumn, the season that casts a romantic melancholy over many of his poems. As Davis moved from poetry to fiction, and from sketches and short stories to novels, this preoccupation with autumn disappears and spring becomes steadily more prominent in his writing and more thoroughly integrated into the development of his stories and novels. In *Winds of Morning*, it has become an essential part of the novel; this change indicates Davis's steadily developing affirmation which he uses nature to express.

V   *The Basic Themes: Initiation and Alienation*

Through the long span of Davis's examination of the Western experience, a few major themes emerge that lie at the root of man's experience and unite it to the universal human condition throughout the world and throughout history. In fact, our understanding of these themes and of how they function in Davis's writing is the key to our fullest appreciation of Davis's artistic achievement. These thematic patterns can be summarized in six general categories: initiation, alienation, Christian patterns of sin, atonement, and redemption, the costs and meanings of love, illusion and aspiration, and the proper uses of the past.

Initiation themes, which present the development of new understanding on the part of a central character, and which occur frequently in Davis's fiction, usually involve a "father-son" conflict between an old man and a boy in his late teens.[9] In our youth-oriented society, such a conflict is not uncommon in our literature, but Davis's treatment has notable differences. Since we have observed most of these differences in examining the various individual works, they need only to be summarized here.

First, the initiation that resolves the father-son conflict involves new knowledge and deeper understanding on the part of both, not just the initiation of the youngster. Second, the positions of the two are usually reversed from the traditional association of age with experience and youth with unrealistic idealism; for, in Davis's work, the older man is usually the innocent idealist and the boy is the cynical voice of worldly experience. In "Open Winter," for example, old Apling insists on idealistic devotion to a task that appears impossible, beyond any obligation, and completely profitless. Beech Cartwright, the boy, is the realist who knows the task is both hopeless and worthless. He also understands the hostility to be expected from the sheep outfits, but Apling expects openness and fairness from them in sharing the range. Although the final initiation of driving the horses into the river town is Beech's, old Apling has lost, in the process of getting there, his innocent trust in the unvarying good will of humanity. As Apling comments, they then make a team. Similar patterns of dual initiation occur in "The Homestead Orchard" and in *Winds of Morning*.

Davis also makes use of the more traditional simple, single initiation theme in *Honey in the Horn* as well as in such short stories as "The Stubborn Spearmen" and "Extra Gang." In these, a boy in late adolescence or early manhood, perhaps one isolated from society, has an experience that helps him understand more fully the faults as well as the virtues of the people around him; and, with such understanding, he accepts them and joins society. In each case the initiation is an affirmative experience, even though it may have been accompanied by some kind of loss of innocence. The experience never ends, however, with the defeated protagonist's walking away from society, alone, through the gray rain. Initiation for Davis is invariably an experience that ends isolation and brings the initiate into human society.

The theme of alienation is frequently associated with the use of initiation in Davis's fiction but not in the poetry. Nonetheless, the speaker in many of Davis's poems is an alienated observer of society who remains statically isolated. In the later fiction, however, the development of the plot brings an end to the central character's isolation and he finds ways to rejoin the human community.

For example, the *pícaro* of Davis's fiction may easily be isolated from the society through which he travels but in which he has no fixed home, as is the case with Clay Calvert in *Honey in the Horn* and with Amos Clarke and old Hendricks in *Winds of Morning*. Ruhama and Askwani in *Beulah Land* have to find both their place in society and their acceptance and understanding of love. Caught between white society and Indian society, they, too, end their alienation with new understanding. Similar patterns occur in some of the short stories, but the wife in "Old Man Isbell's Wife" does not so much end her isolation from society as rise above not only her isolation but also the society from which she is excluded.

VI *Love and Christian Symbolism*

Underlying these patterns of initiation and of alienation is the basic human need for love. Every one of Davis's novels and the majority of his poems deal with the question in some significant way. Clay's love for Luce makes it possible for him to accept human society with all its guilt upon it in *Honey in the Horn*. Love is one of the three driving motives both for Tallien and for the three Americans in *Harp of a Thousand Strings*. Every variety of love—love of land, love for one's own people, love between parent and child, and love between man and woman—is explored in *Beulah Land*. The risk of each in terms of vulnerability to losses is shown to be high, but the value of love in giving meaning to life is higher.

In *Winds of Morning,* love is the important affirmation, both for Hendricks and for Amos, as the key to an acceptable future and to a meaningful acceptance of the past. Hendricks finally has to accept the full scope and meaning of his love for his daughter and, in his acceptance, his love prevails over past alienation from his children. Amos's love for Calanthe gives some value to what he has learned from Hendricks. Both Hendricks and Amos end their alienation from human society because of their acceptance of the significance of love.

In *The Distant Music*, Davis explores what happens to people when the love of land, a special piece of land, becomes the most significant emotion. As a result, love between parent and child, between man and woman, between individual and community are subordinated, lost, or rejected. Only the Inman sisters, kept on the periphery through most of the story, explore and learn the value of other kinds of love; and, in the end, Lydia, not Ransom Mulock, is fulfilled.

Exploration of the forms and consequences of love emerges as a major pattern in all of Davis's longer fiction. From the examination of the working of romantic love between Clay and Luce, this exploration broadens into more subtle and complex considerations of the other common forms human love can take. As Davis's art matured, he came to the fullest and most complex examination of the various forms in *Winds of Morning*. In each case, the novel concludes with a fulfillment and acceptance of the cost of love in pain and sacrifice. Finally, in *The Distant Music*, Davis turned to an examination of a distorted, incomplete, sterile love, but he was only partially successful. We can only speculate where this line of exploration might have carried him had he been able to continue it.

Exploring the deeper levels of human love leads Davis directly to the use of the central symbols and images of Christianity. Through the patterns of sin as a denial of love, atonement through knowledge, and redemption through acceptance, Davis is able to move to the heart of human experience and to unite the life of the American West to the stream of development of Western civilization. These archetypal Christian patterns are so useful that it is no coincidence that they form the structural core of Davis's two finest novels, *Honey in the Horn* and *Winds of Morning*.

Beyond the natural affinity between the problems of human love and the traditional symbolic patterns of Christianity, Davis finds other values in the use of Christian archetypes. The short, direct history of the American West lacks the kinds of cultural associations and allusive context so important to the serious artist. Not only is this regional history short in time, but also in numbers of people and in scope of events. The artist working with Western materials does not have the rise and fall of empires, the fully developed mythologies of a long past, nor the works of centuries of great artists on which to draw. To supply this lack and this need, Davis tried to reestablish the roots of the West in the civilizations from which its people came; and, in this effort, Christianity provided a valuable resource. As a result, his use of the Christian context seems to have grown less from his personal background—although it was present in the person of his Grandfather Bridges—than from his strong sense of the cultural tradition. The vision of the Edenic West, and, in Davis's generation, a sense of the loss of Eden and the hope for redemption through love and suffering, were deeply ingrained folk images ready made in Davis's material. He had only to see their value and shape them to his artistic uses.

From the earliest settlements on the East Coast, the westering settlers themselves saw the occupation of North America in biblical terms, as demonstrated by the biblical names that dot the American landscape from coast to coast. In such patterns as biblical names the materials of the Christian story were available to Western writers. The one essential requirement for such use of Christian elements, of course, is that the writer consistently approach his subjects from a basis of moral obligation. A writer not working within a moral context that assumes freedom of will, with its possibilities for sin, atonement, and redemption, could hardly make use of Christian patterns, nor would he be able to examine the hazards and rewards of love to the depth to which Davis considers them. Consequently, despite his irony and nonsentimentality, despite his detachment from the fates of his characters, H. L. Davis is a moralistic writer who is concerned not only with what people actually do but also with what they ought to do and with what they try to do. His leap from realism to romance lies in his presentation of people who finally solve moral problems, see what they *ought* to do, and then choose to do it in spite of the cost. This leap carries Davis's use of Christian symbolism to the very root of his work.

VII   *Illusion and Aspiration*

Any fictional treatment of the American West that is true to the human experience inevitably has to deal with illusion and aspiration, for both played major roles in bringing people to the West, and the loss of illusion and aspiration was a problem for those who remained or who came during following generations. As a "realist" who does not sentimentalize either the settlers or the Indians, Davis might be expected to favor the destruction of illusion and to scoff at aspirations based on illusions. Such an attitude, of course, is not the case.

The special double-initiation pattern that Davis uses is made possible by the peculiar circumstance, already noted, in which the first generation of settlers were the idealists who expected more of the West and of themselves than either could ever achieve. The later generations were the disenchanted, the cynics who had witnessed the failure of the dreams of their fathers and grandfathers and who had thereby become the often harsh realists. This difference produced the inverted relationship with which Davis worked so effectively: the idealistic, essentially innocent old-timer, still clinging to shreds of the Adamic expectations with which he had entered this Eden; and the cynical youngster for whom aspiration and illusion were the same folly.

That neither view was sufficient is repeatedly the conclusion of the double initiation in Davis's fiction. Uncle Preston Shively and Old Man Isbell are so locked in the past that they are largely irrelevant to the present or the future, and the first Ransom Mulock is so deeply wounded by the betrayals of the past that he cannot even survive the avenging of his wound. But old Apling and old Hendricks are still able to bring the lessons of the past to bear on the present and, at the same time, to learn from the present and modify their understanding of the past.

Their young counterparts, Beech Cartwright, Clay Calvert, and Amos Clarke, help the old-timers learn and modify; and they themselves learn from the old-timers' experience. The result is a convergence of lines of understanding. The conclusion at which they meet retains the value of illusion and of aspiration even when such aspiration is based on illusion. The difference is that the illusion of Adamic isolation and complete independence of action is lost. Aspiration that is retained, despite recognition of the necessary interrelationship of mankind, and of man's infinite capacity for foolishness and evil, becomes heroic. Aspiration based on the illusion of independence and Edenic perfectibility is only foolish.

Old Hendricks reiterates, as we have often noted, that what a man puts into life is more important than what he gets out; and he continues in that belief after his full initiation into the reality of the present. In Davis's fiction, this view is the one which the old idealist and the young cynic finally share. In effect, even failure, if it is due to worthy aspiration, and if it is met with dignity and courage, is not really failure at all. Remaining faithful to worthy aspiration—living, as old Hendricks suggests, according to one's sentiments—is in itself sufficient success regardless of the outcome.

From the position of the old-timer, this means accepting the likelihood of failure without becoming discouraged. From the point of view of the cynical youth, this means paying less attention to what is possible, or even likely, and focusing on what is worth the efforts of a man's life. In short, we find ourselves back at the moral center of Davis's work: doing that which one ought to do is more satisfying than doing that at which one can always succeed.

VIII   Connecting Past and Present

In choosing to write about the American West, H. L. Davis accepted a number of handicaps, and one of the largest of these was a paradox. Not only does the West have a very short past, with little of the allusive richness so important to an artist, but also whatever past the West does have has been so stereotypically mythologized that it is almost unusable by a serious writer of fiction. Furthermore, one of the effects of this distortion of the Western past has been to isolate it from any present reality. To the average modern consciousness, Jim Bridger and Matt Dillon have equal reality, and neither has any more relevance to the present society of western Kansas or western Wyoming in the latter half of the twentieth century than King Arthur or Lancelot. As Davis observed in 1954, "All the new changes in the country, its overgrown towns, its leveled forests and stopped-up creeks, its swarms of new faces and jangle of strange accents, are a consequence of something that has happened somewhere."[10] The modern Westerner has too often lost a sense of real connection with the past, although such a connection does exist.

The problem of the grandiose landscape, which we have already examined, must also be avoided or surmounted by writers who use the West's real past. Davis overcame this problem by most often examining the foreground rather than the broader panorama. With his wry, unsentimental irony he has avoided mysticism and has kept the focus on the real affairs of real people, not on giants who match the giant terrain. As he looks at the history of the region, he does not allow even the first explorers and settlers to assume the gigantic proportions of their total accomplishment.

Most important in establishing a usable past for the West, and in making it a usable setting for serious writers, Davis has established that the West has a real history that is not isolated; for it is related not only to the West's present but also to all of human history. Western settlers did not just begin to exist when they arrived in the

West; they brought with them the whole history, experience, wisdom, foolishness, and other elements of the cultural heritage of people from all parts of the world. The experience of the West is part and parcel of the whole experience of mankind.

Davis establishes this concept of continuity in a variety of ways. In *Harp of a Thousand Strings*, Davis demonstrates it in the threads of human story that tie together the events and people of the French Revolution with the establishment of a pioneer town on the Western prairie of America, and it is stated explicitly in the text of the novel. More pervasively throughout Davis's work, the same concept is implied in the underlying patterns that suggest parallels between characters and events in the novels and short stories and in ancient patterns of human experience. The extended use of Christian symbolism is the most obvious illustration of such parallelism, but others exist.

For example, much of the folklore, such as the expression "honey in the horn," probably did not originate in the West. These expressions of the folk experience came from back East, and very likely in many cases from Europe. The uses of team bells, the legendary skills of the teamsters, the dripping of blood in the attic for an unavenged ghost, and many more are clearly older than the history of white settlement in the West. Folklore is perhaps one of the most authentic testimonials to the commonality of human experience throughout the world and throughout time. Moreover, other comparisons are not hard to find. The experiences of the Inmans on the deserts of southeast Oregon are much like the experiences of Marco Polo in the deserts of Asia, and the story of Sorefoot Capron is both Promethean and Oedipal.

Davis's task, ultimately, was to bridge the gap described by Wallace Stegner in *Wolf Willow*. When reflecting on his formal education, and comparing it with his folk education as a child in the Canadian prairie town of Whitemud, Stegner discovered a major discontinuity. To Stegner, the folk skills of any frontier are primitive and universal: "you cannot tell a Norwegian from a Dukhobor, or either one from an Ontario man . . . our way with simple hand tools, our way with animals, the simpler forms of social organization."[11] Yet in such frontier towns the school system "superimposes five thousand years of Mediterranean culture and two thousand years of Europe upon the adapted or rediscovered simplicities of a new continent" (24). History for Western schoolchildren was what happened in the East or in Europe;

literature was what was written in the past in England. As a consequence, the frontier existed for these people as a disconnected present that was related to nothing that had gone before or that existed
elsewhere. The traditional educational fare of the schools failed to
correct this impression by relating these materials to the time and to
the place of the recently settled West. Such deculturation of the
frontier, Stegner says, means recourse to oral traditions, to folk
tales, music, poetry, and other lore easily memorized (26).

This discontinuity was one of consciousness, not of fact, however.
The frontier community was the product of what had gone before;
it was not *sui generis* there on the prairie or in the mountains.
Stegner's image is of history as a pontoon bridge: "Every man walks
and works at its building end, and has come as far as he has over the
pontoons laid by others he may never have heard of Events have a
way of making other events inevitable; the actions of men are con-
secutive and indivisible" (29).

H. L. Davis's task as a writer in and about the West was to close
this gap in the consciousness of Americans by awakening them to
the continuity of their history and their cultural development. He
shows us that an understanding of our past is necessary for a healthy
sense of community in the present and, therefore, that the West
must not be overwooded and underrooted like Uncle Preston's apple trees, lest we blow over in every strong wind. Davis ac-
complishes this task by building on the felt cultural tradition of the
West, the folk materials of the oral tradition already present in the
consciousness of the people. With this base, he reaches across the
gap in the Western consciousness and finds the connections in the
formal traditions, the unities with events in the formal histories, the
connections with the formal cultural heritage. The Christian tradition proves especially effective in this respect because, of all the
elements of the formal European cultural tradition, Christianity was
the one that survived the deculturation of the frontier. It provided
the connection between the surviving folk knowledge and the
thousands of years of European and Mediterranean culture that is as
much the heritage of Americans as of Europeans.

By showing the unity of Western folk tradition with the experience of all humanity, Davis built the necessary cultural bridge.
By persisting in writing significant literary works using Western
materials, in spite of critical prejudices to the contrary, Davis was
one of a few twentieth-century American writers who have opened

the West for literary settlement and given us back our essential cultural unity. In this effort, H. L. Davis was an original; he did not follow any established "school" or ideology in his writing. He stayed clear of literary cliques and politics; he found his own subjects and developed his own special style for dealing with them. Yet, at the same time, he was deeply aware of the whole cultural tradition of our society and was able to make rich, meaningful use of it. As a result, his work is a significant advance for the American literary tradition.

Notes and References

Chapter One

1. There appears to be no formal record of the date of his birth, but Davis's military service records show this to be the date, and his brother Quentin has personally confirmed the year and place of Harold's birth. Davis gave this date in early biographical material sent to Harriet Monroe; and, in an August 22, 1958, entry in his journal, he gives "Roane's" Mill as his place of birth. Rone's Mill has since disappeared as a recognizable community.

2. Journal entry for January 9, 1957. All journals cited are on deposit in the Humanities Research Library at the University of Texas, Austin.

3. This account is given by Quentin Davis as part of the family tradition. Certainly this jibes with the step-grandfather mentioned in Davis's poetry.

4. Editorial notes, *American Mercury* (April 1930), p. xxvi. Confirmed by Quentin Davis.

5. So far as I have been able to determine, no copies of that newspaper have survived.

6. *The Crimson and Gray*, Senior 1912 Number, Volume IV, No. VIII, The Dalles High School. The Class Will is on pp. 5 - 6; the Class Prophecy, on pp. 7 - 9.

7. In later years, he said that he had been a student at Stanford, leaving to enlist in the army at the beginning of World War I; but Stanford records do not show any enrollment by Harold Davis. The account given here, which is that of his brother Quentin, corresponds more closely with the verifiable records.

8. R. Jeffers, *The Selected Letters of Robinson Jeffers*, ed. Ann N. Ridgeway (Baltimore, 1968), p. 124.

9. See James Stevens, "Bunk-Shanty Ballads and Tales," *Oregon Historical Quarterly*, L (1949), pp. 235 - 42. Stevens says he and Davis wrote "The Frozen Logger," p. 241. Two letters from Davis to Stewart Holbrook, dated January 5 and January 21, 1929, from Westimber, Oregon, are my only evidence of the planing-mill job. These are in the Holbrook collection of the University of Washington Library.

10. Journal for period August 5 to December 12, 1931. Individual entry is not dated.

11. Most of the information concerning the stay in Tennessee was very kindly supplied by novelist Bowen Ingram, who met the Davises during

their time in Lebanon and who continued a correspondence with Harold until a few years before his death. Harold's letters to her and her memorandum of the Davises' time in Tennessee are on deposit in the special collections of the library of the University of Oregon in Eugene. Copies of the letters are also on deposit at the University of Texas and in the Tennessee State Library and Archives.

12. Ingram memorandum.

13. Anon., "Davis Bars Trip Here," *New York Times*, May 10, 1936, p. 27.

14. Letter to Ingram, July 12, 1947, in Oregon collection.

15. Davis's April 23, 1947, letter to Ingram is the earliest reference apparently in Davis's papers. At that time, he was working for Columbia Pictures; but later references indicate he also at times worked for Paramount. I have been unable to determine that any of the scripts on which he worked were actually produced. Earlier, he may also have done research for film scripts.

16. In a May 10, 1950, letter to Ingram, for example, he says he has just recovered from a serious heart illness. A June 2, 1952, entry in his journal says he is chronically ill with anemia.

17. Ferril says he was not, in his essay "I Hate Thursday," *I Hate Thursday* (New York, 1946), pp. 1 - 9. Ferril refers to Davis's contributions, pp. 5 - 6.

18. Discussed and summarized in Davis's journal, entry for August 25, 1955.

19. Letter to Rolstyn Bridges, May 8, 1960, on deposit at the Douglas County Museum, Roseburg, Oregon.

Chapter Two

1. Harriet Monroe, *A Poet's Life: Seventy Years in a Changing World* (New York, 1938), p. 423.

2. *Ibid.*

3. *Ibid.*

4. *Poetry*, XIV (1919), pp. 1 - 2. *Proud Riders* (New York, 1942), p. 63. Hereafter, those poems appearing in the later volume will be cited in their first place of publication and then the pages in the collected volume cited as *PR*, if the poem appears there.

5. *Ibid.*, XIV (1919), pp. 2 - 3. *PR* p. 13 as "Running Vines."

6. *Ibid.*, XIV (1919), p. 3. *PR* p. 5.

7. *Ibid.*, XIV (1919), pp. 4 - 5. *PR* pp. 27 - 28.

8. *Ibid.*, XIV (1919), pp. 5 - 6. *PR* pp. 30 - 31.

9. *Ibid.*, XIV (1919), pp. 6 - 7. *PR* p. 32.

10. *Ibid.*, XIV (1919), pp. 7 - 8. *PR* pp. 24 - 25.

11. *Ibid.*, XIV (1919), pp. 8 - 10. *PR* pp. 43 - 44.

12. *Ibid.*, XIV (1919), pp. 10 - 11. *PR* p. 35.

13. *Ibid.*, XIV (1919), pp. 11 - 12.

14. *Ibid.*, XIV (1919), pp. 12 - 13.

15. Alfred Kreymborg, *Our Singing Strength: An Outline of American Poetry (1620 - 1930)* (New York, 1929), p. 478.

16. Francis F. Greiner, "Voices of the West: Harold L. Davis," *Oregon Historical Quarterly*, LXVI (1965), p. 241.

17. "Others Again," *Poetry*, XVII (1920), p. 151.

18. *Poetry*, XVI (1920), pp. 121 - 22. *PR* p. 14.

19. *Ibid.*, XVI (1920), pp. 124 - 25. *PR* pp. 9 - 10.

20. *Ibid.*, XVI (1920), pp. 125 - 27. *PR* 22 - 23.

21. *Ibid.*, XXI (1922), p. 19. *PR* p. 15.

22. *Ibid.*, XVI (1920), pp. 117 - 19. *PR* pp. 81 - 82.

23. *Ibid.*, XVI (1920), pp. 122 - 23. *PR* p. 21.

24. *Ibid.*, XVI (1920), p. 127. *PR* p. 36.

25. *Ibid.*, XXI (1922), p. 18.

26. *Ibid.*, XXV (1925), pp. 290 - 92. *PR* pp. 18 - 20.

27. *Ibid.*, XXV (1925), p. 296. *PR* p. 16.

28. *Ibid.*, XXV (1925), pp. 298 - 300. *PR* p. 8.

29. *Ibid.*, XXV (1925), pp. 293 - 95. *PR* pp. 6 - 7.

30. *American Mercury*, IX (1926), pp. 323 - 24. *PR* pp. 3 - 4.

31. *Poetry*, XXIX (1927), pp. 177 - 85. *PR* pp. 56 - 62.

32. George C. Shaw, *The Chinook Jargon and How to Use It* (Seattle, 1919), p. 17, defines *nanitsh* as a verb meaning to *see, look, look for*. Davis, however, uses the word as a noun. Citing Davis as his authority, H. L. Mencken, *The American Language* (New York, 1949), pp. 150 - 151, defines *nanitch* as a journey. In this context, "White Petal Nanitch" suggests a journey through spring, the time of blossoming.

33. *Poetry*, XXXII (1928), pp. 299 - 302. *PR* pp. 84 - 86.

34. *Ibid.*, XXXII (1928), pp. 302 - 303. *PR* pp. 45 - 46.

35. *Ibid.*, XXXII (1928), pp. 303 - 304. *PR* pp. 64 - 65.

36. *American Mercury*, XVI (1929), pp. 94 - 95. *PR* pp. 53 - 55.

37. B. A. Botkin, ed., *Folk-Say: A Regional Miscellany* (Norman, Oklahoma, 1930), pp. 137 - 39.

38. *Frontier*, X (1930), pp. 187 - 91. *PR* pp. 66 - 73.

39. *Poetry*, XLII (1933), pp. 68 - 69. *PR* pp. 33 - 34.

40. *Ibid.*, XLII (1933), pp. 61 - 67. *PR* pp. 47 - 52.

41. *Proud Riders* (New York, 1942), p. 39.

42. *Ibid.*, pp. 74 - 80.

43. *Ibid.*, p. 83.

44. Warren L. Clare, " 'Poets, Parasites, and Pismires,' *Status Rerum*, by James Stevens and H. L. Davis," *Pacific Northwest Quarterly*, LXI (1970), pp. 22 - 23.

45. Jeffers, *The Selected Letters . . .*, p. 177.

46. This aspect of Davis's poetry is discussed briefly by Sara Henderson Hay in her review of *Proud Riders* in *Saturday Review of Literature*, XXV

(August 15, 1942), p. 15. In "A Hill Come Out of the Sea," Davis acknowledges this technique: "Here I would invent praise, and have learned no other than to name / The kinds of grass here."

47. Davis, n.d., journal in the University of Texas collection at Austin, p. 349. All references to Davis's journals are to those at the University of Texas.

48. In a letter dated June 2, 1926, to Harriet Monroe, *Selected Letters*, p. 76.

49. "A New Englander," *Poetry*, XVII (1921), p. 344.

50. "Jeffers Denies Us Twice," *Poetry*, XXXI (1928), p. 279. This is a review of *The Women at Point Sur*.

51. Journal for January 25, 1957.

Chapter Three

1. Jeffers, *The Selected Letters . . .*, p. 94. This is in a letter to Harriet Monroe, November 26, 1928.

2. "Jeffers Denies Us Twice," *Poetry*, XXXI (1928), p. 279.

3. *New York Times Book Review*, February 7, 1954, pp. 1, 17.

4. *Kettle of Fire* (New York, 1959), pp. 13 - 18. Further references to works in this volume will have page numbers in parentheses.

5. "Occidental's Prodigal" and "Oleman Hattie" were published in 1928 in the April 1 and July 15 issues of *Adventure* magazine, pp. 137 - 54 and 122 - 34, respectively. They were written in collaboration with James Stevens and published under Stevens's name alone, according to Davis's brother Quentin. Professor Richard Etulain has interviewed Stevens on the subject, and he reports that Stevens gave the same account.

6. Davis's journal for the late 1950s (in the library of the University of Texas at Austin) contains notes developing this story. These notes indicate that he had probably not worked on this story any earlier.

7. The ten I would select are: "Old Man Isbell's Wife" (1929), "Flying Switch" (1930), "Shiloh's Waters" (1930), "Extra Gang" (1931), "Hell to Be Smart" (1935), "Beach Squatter" (1936), "Open Winter" (1939), "The Homestead Orchard" (1939), "A Flock of Trouble" (1941), and "The Kettle of Fire" (1959). Full reference to all of these is given in the bibliography of Davis's work.

8. Pare Lorentz, Jr., "H. L. Davis: A Portrait of the West." Unpublished honors thesis, Harvard College, March 2, 1959.

9. *Team Bells Woke Me* (New York, 1953), pp. 255 - 56. Further references to works in this volume will have page numbers in parentheses.

10. Undated letter apparently written before 1941 in the Davis papers at the University of Texas.

11. Perhaps it is drawing the symbolism out too far to observe that Radford's initials, D. R., suggest Deus Rex, but it does fit the rest of the pattern.

12. *Team Bells*, pp. x - xi.

13. Journal, June 12, 1946, p. 33.

14. *Ibid.*

15. Phillip Jones, "The West of H. L. Davis," *South Dakota Review*, VI (1968 - 69), pp. 77 - 78.

Chapter Four

1. Davis's journal for the period from August 5 through December 12, 1931, contains these and other references to his early efforts to get his first novel started. The entries are not dated and the pages are not numbered. His journals are on deposit at the Humanities Research Library at the University of Texas in Austin.

2. *Honey in the Horn* (New York, 1935), p. 38. All subsequent page references in text are to this edition.

3. Davis discusses this at length in his journal entries between August 5 and December 12, 1931.

4. William Plomer, *Spectator*, CLV (1935), p. 334.

5. Mary McCarthy, "Tall Timber," *The Nation*, CXLI (1935), pp. 248 - 49.

6. Cowley's review is in "Oregon Trail," *The New Republic*, LXXXIV (September 4, 1935), p. 107. His rebuke of Mary McCarthy is in "Two Items for Reference," *The New Republic*, LXXXV (December 25, 1935), p. 203.

7. Letter to Mildred Bowen Ingram, February 10, 1955, now in the University of Oregon Library.

8. Davis's journal for the period August 5 to December 12, 1931. No specific date is attached to this entry, but it was probably in August.

9. Clifton Fadiman, "Books: A Prize Novel and a Good One," *The New Yorker*, XI (August 24, 1935), pp. 52 - 54.

10. Robert Penn Warren, "Some Recent Novels," *The Southern Review*, I (1936), pp. 639 - 41.

11. Davis's journal, February 8, 1936.

12. H. L. Mencken, *Letters*, ed. Guy J. Forgue (New York, 1961), p. 394.

13. Letter to Davis, May 17, 1939, in *Letters of H. L. Mencken*, p. 436.

14. For example, see W. Tasker Witham, *The Adolescent in the American Novel, 1920 - 60* (New York, 1964), pp. 94, 190 - 91, 261; W. J. Stuckey, *The Pulitzer Prize Novels* (Norman, Oklahoma, 1966), pp. 24, 104.

15. For example, see Phillip L. Jones, "The West of H. L. Davis," *South Dakota Review*, VI (1968 - 69), pp. 72 - 84; Dayton Kohler, "H. L. Davis: Writer in the West," *College English*, XIV (1952), pp. 133 - 40; Jan Brunvand, "*Honey in the Horn* and 'Acres of Clams': The Regional Fiction of H. L. Davis," *Western American Literature*, II (1967), pp. 135 - 40; Francis F. Greiner, "Voice of the West: Harold L. Davis," *Oregon Historical Quarterly*, LXVI (1965), pp. 240 - 48.

16. For one instance of this judgment, see Ellis Lucia, *This Land Around Us: A Treasury of Pacific Northwest Writing* (Garden City, New York, 1969), p. xxi.

17. Letter to Mildred Bowen Ingram, February 10, 1955. In the library of the University of Oregon.

18. The comparison was first discussed by John Lauber, "A Western Classic: H. L. Davis's *Honey in the Horn*," *The Western Humanities Review*, XVI (1962), pp. 85 - 86.

19. Journal for April 3, 1957.

Chapter Five

1. Even later critics, such as Dayton Kohler, "H. L. Davis: Writer in the West," *College English*, XLI (1952), pp. 133 - 40, regard this novel primarily as a historical novel or as a "period piece," while at the same time recognizing its complexity and "patient craftsmanship."

2. Examples of some of these reviews of *Harp* would include Joseph Henry Jackson, "Contrived Corridors," *San Francisco Chronicle* (November 19, 1947), p. 14; Thomas Hornsby Ferril, "Ideas and Comments," *Rocky Mountain Herald*, LXXXVII (June 14, 1947), p. 1; James Hilton, *New York Herald Tribune Weekly Book Review* (November 2, 1947), p. 4.

3. Letter to Bowen Ingram, September 23, 1945, now in the University of Oregon Library.

4. Walter Blair, ed., *Native American Humor* (San Francisco, 1960), pp. 388 - 89.

5. *Poetry*, XXXI (1928), p. 277.

6. Thomas Hornsby Ferril, "Ideas and Comments," *The Rocky Mountain Herald*, LXXXVII, 44 (November 1, 1947), pp. 1 - 2.

7. Pare Lorentz, Jr., "H. L. Davis: A Portrait of the West," unpublished honors thesis, Harvard College, March 2, 1959, quotes a letter from Davis to his editor in which Davis mentions the conflicts between man and nature and man and society as being illustrated by the three Americans. He apparently did not mention the struggle of man against himself, although it also appears in the novel.

Chapter Six

1. *Beulah Land* (New York, 1949), pp. 56 - 61. All page references are to this edition.

2. Useful examples of such reviews are Dale L. Morgan, "Fusing Red and White Cultures," *Saturday Review of Literature*, XXXII (June 11, 1949), pp. 15, 29; Hamilton Basso, "The Great Open Spaces," *The New Yorker*, XXV (June 4, 1949), pp. 84, 87 - 88; E. F. Walbridge, *Library Journal*, LXXIV (May 15, 1949), p. 818.

3. Davis's journal for September 6, 1953. This entry was written before *The Distant Music,* Davis's final novel, but it seems unlikely that Davis would have preferred it over *Beulah Land.* In any case, he clearly rated this novel highly.

4. The whole account of Davis's intentions with *Beulah Land,* and of his evaluation of how well he succeeded in accomplishing them, is in this journal entry for April 17, 1953.

5. Henry James discusses this in his preface to *The American.* See *The Art of the Novel,* ed. R. P. Blackmur (New York, 1953), pp. 25 - 37.

Chapter Seven

1. For examples of this kind of review, see Howard Mumford Jones's review, *Saturday Review,* XXXV (January 19, 1952), pp. 16 - 17; also Oscar Lewis, *New York Herald Tribune Book Review* (January 6, 1952), p. 3; Margaret Marshall, *Nation,* CLXXIV (February 2, 1952), p. 110; also anonymous reviews in *U.S. Quarterly Book Review,* VII (1952), p. 137; *Time,* LIX (January 7, 1952), p. 90.

2. Edward Weeks referred to the novel as Americana in his review in *Atlantic,* CLXXXIX (February 1952), p. 78. Margaret Marshall in the *Nation* review (already cited) praised the language. The anonymous reviewer in *Newsweek,* XXXIX (January 14, 1952), p. 84, called it "a truly western story," without making at all clear what that means.

3. Anon., *New York Times Book Review* (January 6, 1952), p. 5.

4. *Winds of Morning* (New York, 1952). Page references are to this edition.

5. This acceptance scene is discussed by Dayton Kohler, "H. L. Davis: Writer in the West," *College English,* XIV (1952), p. 138.

6. Brief treatments of the Lilith myth may be found in Theodor H. Gaster, *Myth, Legend, and Custom in the Old Testament* (New York, 1969), pp. 578 - 80; W. S. Walsh, *Heroes and Heroines of Fiction Classical, Medieval, Legendary* (Philadelphia, 1966), p. 175.

7. A useful discussion of Davis's use of folk materials may be found in Kirk Martin Hegbloom, "Theme and Folklore in H. L. Davis' *Winds of Morning,*" unpublished master's thesis, University of Idaho, 1968. I am indebted to Mr. Hegbloom for some of the insights presented here.

8. This aspect of the use of folk materials has been perceptively discussed by Phillip L. Jones, "The West of H. L. Davis," *South Dakota Review,* VI (1968 - 69), pp. 72 - 84. For this specific plot, see particularly p. 73.

9. An entry in Davis's journal for April 26, 1949, indicates that from the early stages of his writing of the novel, he saw old Hendricks as a quixotic figure modeled on Davis's grandfather.

10. I have dealt in some detail with this theme in "H. L. Davis: Viable Uses for the Past," *Western American Literature,* III (1968), pp. 3 - 18.

Chapter Eight

1. At his death in 1960, Davis was at work on a novel with the working title, "Exit, Pursued by a Bear." The manuscript of that work is in the Davis collection at the Humanities Research Library at the University of Texas in Austin.

2. "A Town in Eastern Oregon," *American Mercury*, XIX (1930), pp. 75 - 83. The sketch was later included in *Team Bells Woke Me* (New York, 1953), pp. 173 - 91.

3. *Team Bells Woke Me* (New York, 1953), pp. x - xii.

4. See for example J. A. Burns, *Library Journal*, LXXXII (1957), p. 77; *Booklist*, LIII (1957), p. 297.

5. Walter Havighurst, *New York Herald Tribune Book Review*, (February 3, 1957), p. 5.

6. Anon., *Booklist*, LIII (1957), p. 297.

7. Carl Carmer, "Tragicomic Dance," *Saturday Review of Literature*, XL (March 2, 1957), pp. 15 - 16.

8. Walter Van Tilburg Clark, "The Call of the Far Country," *New York Times Book Review* (February 3, 1957), pp. 5, 29.

9. *The Distant Music* (New York, 1957), p. 1. This edition cited in this chapter. Hereafter, citations are by page number within the text.

Chapter Nine

1. F. E. Hodgins, "The Literary Emancipation of a Region: The Changing Image of the American West in Fiction," doctoral dissertation, Michigan State University, 1957, p. 417.

2. Thomas Hornsby Ferril, *Rocky Mountain Herald* (November 5, 1960), p. 1.

3. Wallace Stegner, *Wolf Willow* (New York, 1962), p. 21.

4. Carl Sandburg, "Something About H. L. Davis," *Rocky Mountain Herald* (April 1, 1950), pp. 1 - 2.

5. Davis's letter, dated October 16, 1947, is on deposit in the Humanities Research Library at the University of Texas in Austin.

6. Hodgins, p. 467.

7. This is in Davis's entry in his journal for December 11, 1954.

8. Ferril, "Writing in the Rockies," *Rocky Mountain Reader* (New York, 1946), pp. 395 - 98.

9. One might speculate on the extent to which this frequent use of such a theme grew out of Davis's relationship with his own father. As has already been noted, Davis's journals suggest that his relationship with his father was ambiguous and at least at times strained. Perhaps this frequent perceptive examination of such a theme was Davis's own attempt to resolve his relationship with his father. This would be an interesting and useful question for Davis's biographer.

10. Preface to *Kettle of Fire* (New York, 1959), p. 17.

11. Stegner, *Wolf Willow*, p. 23.

Selected Bibliography

PRIMARY SOURCES

This bibliography of Davis's work has benefited substantially from previous bibliographies, some of which are listed among the secondary sources, but in addition it includes a number of items unlisted in earlier compilations. All of Davis's published writings are listed giving the first place of appearance and, within each category, chronologically in order of first appearance. Later editions, republications, and incorporation in anthologies are not listed.

1. Papers and Manuscripts

The principal collection of Davis's journals, correspondence, and other papers is in the Humanities Research Center, The University of Texas at Austin. Smaller but substantial collections are at the University of Oregon Library and the Tennessee State Library and Archives. Assorted additional material may be found in the Harriet Monroe collection of the Joseph Regenstein Library at the University of Chicago, the Library of the University of Washington in Seattle, and the Douglas County Museum in Roseburg, Oregon.

2. Novels

Honey in the Horn. New York: Harper & Brothers, 1935.
Harp of a Thousand Strings. New York: William Morrow & Company, 1947.
Beulah Land. New York: William Morrow & Company, 1949.
Winds of Morning. New York: William Morrow & Company, 1952.
The Distant Music. New York: William Morrow & Company, 1957.

3. Collections

Proud Riders and Other Poems. New York: Harper & Brothers, 1942.
Team Bells Woke Me and Other Stories. New York: William Morrow & Company, 1953.
Kettle of Fire. New York: William Morrow & Company, 1959.
The Selected Poems of H. L. Davis, with an introduction by Thomas Hornsby Ferril. Boise, Idaho: Ahsahta Press, 1978.

4. Poetry

For groups of poems published together, the poems are listed in the order in which they appeared in the publication. Most of Davis's best poems were collected and published in *Proud Riders and Other Poems,* cited under "Collections." For convenience, those that appear in *Proud Riders* carry, after citation of initial appearance, the additional notation, *PR*, with the page numbers on which they appear in that volume. The last three poems were published only in *Proud Riders.*

"The Sweet Tasting." *Poetry,* XIV (April, 1919), 1 - 2. *PR,* 63.

"Running Vines in a Field." *Poetry,* XIV (April 1919), 2 - 3. *PR* as "Running Vines," 13.

"A Field by the River." *Poetry,* XIV (April 1919), 3. *PR,* 5.

"In the Field." *Poetry,* XIV (April 1919), 4 - 5. *PR,* 27 - 28.

"The Gypsy Girl." *Poetry,* XIV (April 1919), 5 - 6. *PR,* 30 - 31.

"The Spirit." *Poetry,* XIV (April 1919), 6 - 7. *PR,* 32.

"My Step-Grandfather." *Poetry,* XIV (April 1919) 7 - 8. *PR,* 24 - 25.

"Oakland Pier: 1918." *Poetry,* XIV (April 1919), 8 - 10. *PR,* 43 - 44.

"The Old Are Sleepy." *Poetry,* XIV (April 1919), 10 - 11. *PR,* 35.

"Flags." *Poetry,* XIV (April 1919), 11 - 12.

"The Valley Harvest." *Poetry,* XIV (April 1919), 12 - 13.

"In This Wet Orchard." *Poetry,* XVI (June 1920), 117 - 19. *PR,* 81 - 82.

"Stalks of Wild Hay." *Poetry,* XVI (June 1920), 119. *PR,* 26.

"Baking Bread." *Poetry,* XVI (June, 1920), 120 - 21. *PR,* 11 - 12.

"The Rain Crow." *Poetry,* XVI (June 1920), 121 - 22. *PR,* 14.

"The Threshing Floor." *Poetry,* XVI (June 1920), 122 - 23. *PR,* 21.

"From a Vineyard." *Poetry,* XVI (June 1920), 123 - 24. *PR,* 17.

"The Market-Gardens." *Poetry,* XVI (June 1920), 124 - 25. *PR,* 9 - 10.

"October: 'The Old Eyes'." *Poetry,* XVI (June 1920), 125 - 27. *PR,* 22 - 23.

"To the River Beach." *Poetry,* XVI (June 1920), 127. *PR,* 36.

"Open Hands." *Poetry,* XXI (October 1922), 18.

"Dog Fennel." *Poetry,* XXI (October 1922), 19. *PR,* 15.

"Binding Hands." *Poetry,* XXV (March 1925), 289. *PR,* 37.

"Mid-September." *Poetry,* XXV (March 1925), 290 - 92. *PR,* 18 - 20.

"The River People." *Poetry,* XXV (March 1925), 293 - 95. *PR,* 6 - 7.

"The Dead Bird." *Poetry,* XXV (March 1925), 295.

"Renewing Windbreak." *Poetry,* XXV (March 1925), 296. *PR,* 16.

"A Hill Come Out of the Sea." *Poetry,* XXV (March 1925), 297. *PR,* 38.

"The Deep Water." *Poetry,* XXV (March 1925), 298 - 300. *PR,* 8.

"Of the Dead of a Forsaken Country." *American Mercury,* IX (November 1926), 323 - 24. *PR,* 3 - 4.

"White Petal Nanitch." *Poetry,* XXIX (January 1927), 177 - 85. *PR,* 56 - 62.

"Steel Gang." *Poetry,* XXXII (September 1928), 299 - 302. *PR,* 84 - 86.

"Cloudy Day." *Poetry,* XXXII (September 1928), 302 - 303. *PR,* 45 - 46.

"Rivers to Children." *Poetry,* XXXII (September 1928), 303 - 304. *PR,* 64 - 65.

"Crop Campers." *American Mercury,* XVI (January 1929), 94 - 95. *PR,* 53 - 55.

"Threshing Crew Woman." *Folk-Say: A Regional Miscellany.* B. A. Botkin, ed. Norman: University of Oklahoma Press, 1930, 137 - 39.

"Juan Chacon." *Frontier*, X (March 1930), 187 - 91. *PR* as "White Flags," 66 - 73.
"In Argos." *Poetry*, XLII (May 1933), 61 - 67. *PR*, 47 - 52.
"New Birds." *Poetry*, XLII (May 1933), 68 - 69. *PR*, 33 - 34.
"Mountain Autumns," *PR*, 39.
"The Deaf and Dumb Girl," *PR*, 74 - 80.
"Brynhild," *PR*, 83.

5. Short Prose Works

Davis's short prose writings have been divided into groups corresponding to the categories discussed in Chapter 3. The single exception is the separate listing of the very short pieces published over a number of years in the *Rocky Mountain Herald*. These were generally casual, informal notes on a wide variety of subjects.

Many of Davis's best short prose works have been collected in two volumes, *Team Bells Woke Me* and *Kettle of Fire*, cited under "Collections." For convenience, those works that appear in these volumes carry, after the citation of initial appearance, the additional notation *TB* if they appear also in *Team Bells* and *KF* if they appear also in *Kettle of Fire*. Page numbers and, where they occur, variant titles are indicated.

6. Short Stories

Two short stories were published in 1928 under the name of James Stevens which were written by Davis or were the result of collaboration of the two, according to Quentin Davis and confirmed in a letter from Professor Richard Etulain from an interview with James Stevens. Those stories were "Occidental's Prodigal." *Adventure*, LXVI (April 11, 1928), 137 - 54; and "Oleman Hattie." *Adventure*, LXVII (July 15, 1928), 122 - 34.
"Old Man Isbell's Wife." *American Mercury*, XVI (February 1929), 142 - 49. *TB*, 132 - 50.
"The Brown Stallion." *American Mercury*, XVIII (September 1929), 8 - 16.
"Cow-town Widows." *American Mercury*, XVIII (December 1929), 464 - 73.
"Flying Switch." *Collier's*, LXXXVI (August 2, 1930), 14 - 15, 48 - 50. *TB*, 192 - 214.
"Shiloh's Waters." *The Miscellany*, I (September 1930), 26 - 39. *TB*, 215 - 39.
"Wild Horse Siding." *Collier's*, LXXXVIII (October 17, 1931), 14 - 15, 64 - 66.
"Extra Gang." *American Mercury*, XXIV (October 1931), 161 - 70. *TB*, 240 - 59.
"Murder Story." *American Mercury*, XXX (November 1933), 303 - 11.
"Wild Headlight." *Collier's*, XCII (December 30, 1933), 34 - 35, 39 - 40.
"Spanish Lady." *Collier's*, XCIV (July 14, 1934), 7 - 8, 34, 36, 38, 40.

164   H. L. DAVIS

"Shotgun Junction." *Collier's*, XCIV (November 3, 1934), 24, 41 - 43.
"The Vanishing Wolf." *Collier's*, XCV (February 2, 1935), 17, 34 - 35, 38,
    40. *TB*, 260 - 80.
"A Horse for Felipa." *Collier's*, XCV (June 15, 1935), 16 - 17, 58, 60 - 61.
"Railroad Beef." *Collier's*, XCVI (October 19, 1935), 29, 48, 50 - 52, 54.
"Hell To Be Smart." *American Mercury*, XXXVI (November 1935), 292 -
    303.
"Mrs. Almina Steed." *Ladies Home Journal*, LIII (March 1936), 30 - 31,
    134, 136, 138, 140.
"Cowboy Boots." *Saturday Evening Post*, CCIX (August 1, 1936), 12 - 13,
    60 - 62, 64.
"Beach Squatter." *Saturday Evening Post*, CCIX (November 21, 1936),
    18 - 19, 39, 41, 44, 46. *TB*, 58 - 85.
"Open Winter." *Saturday Evening Post*, CCXI (May 6, 1939), 12 - 13, 112,
    114 - 15, 117 - 18, 120. *TB*, 3 - 33.
"The Homestead Orchard." *Saturday Evening Post*, CCXII (July 29, 1939),
    14 - 15, 74 - 76, 78. *TB*, 86 - 111.
"World of Little Doves." *Saturday Evening Post*, CCXIII (April 26, 1941),
    12 - 13, 90, 92, 95, 97 - 98. *TB*, 281 - 300.
"A Flock of Trouble." *Saturday Evening Post*, CCXIV (November 8, 1941),
    24 - 25, 57 - 58, 62, 66 - 67. *TB* as "Stubborn Spearmen," 34 - 57.
"A Sorrel Horse Don't Have White Hoofs." *Saturday Evening Post*,
    CCXIV (December 27, 1941), 14 - 15, 60 - 62, 64.
"The Kettle of Fire." *Northwest Review*, II (Summer 1959), 5 - 22. *KF*,
    165 - 89.

7. Sketches

"The Old-Fashioned Land—Eastern Oregon." *The Frontier*, IX (March
    1929), 201 - 207.
"Back to the Land—Oregon, 1907." *American Mercury*, XVI (March
    1929), 314 - 23. *TB*, 151 - 72.
"A Town in Eastern Oregon." *American Mercury*, XIX (January 1930), 75 -
    83. *TB*, 173 - 91.
"Water on the Wheat." *American Mercury*, XIX (February 1930), 137 - 44.
"Hand-Press Journalist." *American Mercury*, XIX (April 1930), 478 - 86.
"Three Hells: A Comparative Study." *American Mercury*, XX (July 1930),
    257 - 67.
"A Pioneer Captain." *American Mercury*, XXII (February 1931), 149 - 59.
"Team Bells Woke Me." *American Mercury*, XXII (April 1931), 444 - 53.
    TB, 112 - 31.
"The Last Indian Outbreak: 1906." *American Mercury*, XXX (September
    1933), 50 - 57.
"American Apostle." *American Mercury*, XXX (October 1933), 219 - 27.

8. Essays

"Oregon." *Holiday*, XIII (June 1953), 34 - 47, 108, 110, 112 - 13, 115 - 18, 120 - 21. *KF*, 19 - 48.

"Fishing Fever." *Holiday*, XIV (August 1953), 56 - 60, 62. *KF*, 49 - 65.

"The Puget Sound Country." *Holiday*, XV (May 1954), 98 - 105, 117 - 18, 123 - 24, 126 - 28. *KF* as "Puget Sound Country," 79 - 99.

"A Walk in the Woods." *Holiday*, XV (November 1954), 88 - 90, 92 - 93, 95 - 96. *KF*, 66 - 78.

"The Wilds of Mexico." *Holiday*, XXI (May 1957), 26, 31, 33 - 34, 36, 118, 120 - 22.

"The Pleasures of the Brook." *Holiday*, XXII (July 1957), 74 - 75, 98 - 101, 103. *KF* as "The Brook," 100 - 14.

"Palm Springs." *Holiday*, XXII (October 1957), 84 - 85, 97 - 102.

"Our Resourceful Forests." *Holiday*, XXIV (July 1958), 72 - 79, 82 - 83, 86 - 87. *KF* as "The Forests," 131 - 48.

"The Best Time for Camping." *Holiday*, XXIV (September 1958), 78 - 81, 83, 131. *KF* as "The Camp," 115 - 30.

"Sheepherders: The Quiet Westerners." *Holiday*, XXV (May 1959), 19 - 22, 24 - 25, 27. *KF* as "Sheep Herding," 149 - 64.

"Oregon Autumn." *Holiday*, XXX (November 1961), 155 - 56, 173 - 77.

9. Literary Criticism

"A New Englander." *Poetry*, XVII (March 1921), 343 - 44. Review of *The Township Line* by A. F. Wilson.

"Robert Bridges Once More." *Poetry*, XVII (March 1921), 344 - 45. Review of *October and Other Poems* by Robert Bridges.

[With James Stevens]. *Status Rerum: A Manifesto upon the Present Condition of Northwestern Literature Containing Several Near Libelous Utterances upon Persons in the Public Eye*. The Dalles, Oregon: privately printed, 1926.

"Enter the Woman." *Poetry*, XXX (September 1927), 338 - 46. Review of "Ballad of the Singing Bowl," by Marjorie A. Seiffert.

"Jeffers Denies Us Twice." *Poetry*, XXXI (February 1928), 274 - 79. Review of *The Women at Point Sur*, by Robinson Jeffers.

"Status Rerum—Allegro Ma Non Troppo." *The Frontier*, VIII (March 1928), 70.

"Foreword." Thomas Hornsby Ferril. *New and Selected Poems*. New York: Harper & Brothers, 1952, xiii - xvii.

"Bouquets for Mencken." *Nation*, CLXXVII (September 12, 1953), 212.

"The Elusive Trail to the Old West." *New York Times Book Review*, February 7, 1954, 1, 17. *KF* as "Preface: A Look Around," 13 - 18.

"The Range and Vitality of the Frontier West." *New York Times Book*

Review, November 6, 1955, 7, 47. Reviews of *The Frontier Years: L. A. Hoffman, Photographer of the Plains,* by Mark H. Brown and W. R. Patton; *The Settlers' West,* by Martin F. Schmitt and Dee Brown; *The American West,* by Lucius Beebe and Charles Clegg.

"Boy Under the Sky." *New York Times Book Review,* July 15, 1956, 5, 18. Review of *Old Yeller,* by Fred Gipson.

10. *Rocky Mountain Herald* Items

"Westerniana," by Childe Hesperus appeared weekly August 8 - December 26, 1942.

"Hesperiana," by Childe Westerus, somewhat irregularly January 2, 1943 - August 10, 1946. Includes "The Electric Bulldog" in the May 12, 1945, issue.

"The Colonel Discusses Rifles," June 3, 1944, 1.

"Pharmacopoeia Mexicana," June 24, 1944, 1.

"Viva Everything!" August 26, 1944, 1, 7.

"A Note on the Balance of Power," November 4, 1944, 1 - 2.

"On Listening to An Astronomer," November 18, 1944, 1, 8.

"From the Far West," somewhat irregularly June 14, 1947 - January 31, 1953.

"Our Mexican Letter," November 14, 1953, 1 - 2.

"Letter from Mexico," March 12, 1955, 1 - 2; August 6, 1955, 1, 8; August 27, 1955, 1 (appearing in "The Dumb Friends' League" column).

SELECTED SECONDARY SOURCES

ARMSTRONG, GEORGE M. "H. L. Davis's *Beulah Land:* A Revisionist's Novel of Westering," *The Westering Experience in American Literature: Bicentennial Essays,* ed. Merrill Lewis and L. L. Lee. Bellingham, Washington: Western Washington University, 1977. Analyzes Davis's views of the history of the American West.

BAIN, ROBERT. *H. L. Davis.* Boise State University Western Writers Series No. 11. Boise, Idaho: Boise State University, 1974. A critically perceptive overview of Davis's career and his principal works. Includes a bibliography.

BRUNVAND, JAN HAROLD. "*Honey in the Horn* and 'Acres of Clams': The Regional Fiction of H. L. Davis." *Western American Literature,* II (Summer 1967), 135 - 45. Study of Davis's use of folklore, particularly in *Honey in the Horn.*

BRYANT, PAUL T. "H. L. Davis: Viable Uses for the Past." *Western American Literature,* III (Spring 1968), 3 - 18. Effort to show that Davis is a more complex writer than critics have recognized; investigates Davis's techniques for using the past to understand the present.

CLARE, WARREN L. " 'Poets, Parasites, and Pismires,' *Status Rerum,* by

James Stevens and H. L. Davis," *Pacific Northwest Quarterly*, LXI (January 1970), 22 - 30. Summary of effects of *Status Rerum*.

ETULAIN, RICHARD W. "H. L. Davis: A Bibliographical Addendum." *Western American Literature*, V (Summer 1970), 129 - 35. A supplement to the Kellogg bibliography, filling gaps and bringing it up to date. Contains a few errors. Useful.

————. *Western American Literature: A Bibliography of Interpretive Books and Articles*. Vermillion, South Dakota: Dakota Press of the University of South Dakota, 1972. A bibliography of secondary sources on H. L. Davis, 57 - 58.

HEGBLOOM, KIRK MARTIN. "Theme and Folklore in H. L. Davis' *Winds of Morning.*" Unpublished master's thesis, University of Idaho, 1968. Valuable analysis of folklore in Davis's fiction; useful critical analysis of *Winds of Morning.*

HILTON, CHARLES. "A Note on Regionalism." *Northwest Literary Review*, I (September-October 1935), 4. Discusses *Status Rerum* controversy and the value and broader significance of "regional" writers.

HODGINS, FRANCIS EDWARD. "The Literary Emancipation of a Region: The Changing Image of the American West in Fiction." Unpublished doctoral dissertation, Michigan State University, East Lansing, 1957. Relates Davis with other serious modern writers of the West and summarizes Davis's achievement.

JONES, PHILLIP L. "The West of H. L. Davis." *South Dakota Review*, VI (Winter 1968 - 69), 72 - 84. Excellent, wide-ranging discussion of the art of Davis's novels.

KELLOGG, GEORGE. "H. L. Davis, 1896 - 1960: A Bibliography." *Texas Studies in Language and Literature*, V (Summer 1963), 294 - 303. Intended as an exhaustive bibliography, including all editions of Davis's novels and inclusion of Davis's works in anthologies. Lists even minor mention of Davis in secondary sources and includes long but incomplete list of book reviews. Contains a few errors, but is a useful basic bibliographic resource for students of Davis's work.

KOHLER, DAYTON. "H. L. Davis: Writer in the West." *College English*, XIV (December 1952), 133 - 40. First academic critic to recognize Davis's literary achievement. Useful article; still not superseded.

LAUBER, JOHN. "A Western Classic: H. L. Davis's *Honey in the Horn.*" *The Western Humanities Review*, XVI (Winter 1962), 85 - 86. Valuable critical analysis of *Honey in the Horn.* First to see comparison between Huck Finn as not accepting society and Clay Calvert as solving the problem of isolation.

LORENTZ, PARE, JR. "H. L. Davis: A Portrait of the West." Unpublished honors thesis, Harvard College, March 2, 1959. Useful analysis of Davis's literary achievement. Lorentz had the advantage of consulting with Davis in Mexico.

STEVENS, JAMES. " 'Bunk-Shanty Ballads and Tales': The Annual Society

Address." *Oregon Historical Quarterly*, L (December 1949), 235 - 42. Tells of Davis's Washington years and his radio career.

————. "The Northwest Takes to Poesy." *American Mercury*, XVI (January 1929), 64 - 70. Interesting information about Davis's career as a poet in the 1920s.

Index

(The works of Davis are listed under his name.)

169

DEMCO 38-297